# THE DIARY OF A MAD PUBLIC SCHOOL TEACHER

# THE DIARY OF A MAD PUBLIC SCHOOL TEACHER

DAVID A. HANCOCK MA

LIBRARY OF CONGRESS CONTROL NUMBER:      2017910954
ISBN:        HARDCOVER       978-1-5434-3641-9
             SOFTCOVER       978-1-5434-3640-2
             EBOOK           978-1-5434-3639-6

Print information available on the last page.

Rev. date: 07/20/2017

**To order additional copies of this book, contact:**
Xlibris
1-888-795-4274
www.Xlibris.com
Orders@Xlibris.com
759604

I dedicate this collection of letters to the editor to all the students of my teaching and counseling practices as well as to those who are just beginning with their career in teaching and education.

This book is also dedicated to my twenty-thousand-plus students and my inspiring favorite high school teachers—Nancy Lansdowne Knowlton (English) and Hal Burbach (biology/zoology).


## A Gadfly Teacher Monologues

Hancock completed his student teaching in biology at his alma mater in 1968 (a very enlightening experience).

Hancock was also a student in Burbach's health education class at Kent State University (1966–67).

Nancy and Hal proved Henry Adams, who said, "A teacher affects eternity - You can never tell where his/her influence stops."


## Book Title Ideas

White Teacher—Black Students Diabolical
(Letters from an ADHD Mad Public School Teacher)
(Being a White Face in a Black Place)
—Sundry—
Sardonic
Oracular
Satirical
Commentaries
Irascible
Bemused
Reflections
VIPS
Views
Insights

Perspectives
Irascible

This book is about being a white male teacher in a school of black students with many itinerant students.

## DAVID A. HANCOCK, MA

Howland High School Warren, Ohio (1964)

BS Education, biological science / life science 7–12

Health Education 7–12, Kent State University (1968)

MA, John Carroll University (1988)

Educational psychology, school counseling, science education, and professional teaching (1974)

Teacher 7–12—biology, life science, nature study, health; Cleveland Heights-University Heights public schools (1969–2003)

Adjunct professor: education / educational psychology / student-teacher college supervisor / mentor, professional development seminars

Lakeland Community College (1982–1903); Kirtland, Ohio

John Carroll University (1974–1988)

Baldwin Wallace University (2000–2005)

Notre Dame College (2006–2013); South Euclid, Ohio

Lake Erie College ('04, '05, '06); Painesville, Ohio

Brandeis University (1989, 1990, 1995); Waltham, Massachusetts

Awards

Favorite Teachers / TV-8 Teachers of the Week / Funniest Teacher / Most Influential Teacher

Several of Mr. Hancock's students are doctors, nurses, and teachers. One of Mr. Hancock's students performed gallbladder surgery (anesthesiologist), which reminded him of Henry Adams.

*A teacher affects eternity—you can never tell where his/her influence stops.*

# Teaching Philosophy and Style

After thirty-five years of multicultural-classroom teaching experience, I have learned that "we are what we teach." Teaching is a twenty-four-hour-a-day position. We are not teachers just for the time we spend in the classroom or just for the days we spend in school. We are teachers after school, on weekends, and throughout our lives. I entered this profession willingly because I believe in education, and I believe in children, and I believe in the future in which those children will be a part of. If we project that belief in our personal lives, our students cannot help but learn that lesson well. Each of us has within that spark of compassion and concern and love that drove us into teaching in the first place. Each of us can fan that spark into a flame that will warm our classrooms and nurture our students now and in the future.

Also, for me, the hope lies in teaching itself—the hard work requiring ingenuity, patience, and a focus on what is effective with students. At its core, it is not mechanical or technological. I have always thought of myself as a teacher/counselor the way other people think of themselves as gardeners, painters, composers, and poets. I am a craftsperson of learning, working to refine what I do with students for success. I do my best to model my teaching philosophy and style to reflect the writings of William Glasser, Howard Gardner, Herbert Kohl, Neil Postman, Judith Carducci, John Dewey, John Holt, and Charles Silberman.

I constantly keep in mind the indelible words of William Arthur Ward, "The mediocre teacher tells, the good teacher explains, the great teacher inspires," and H. G. Wells, "The future is a race between education and catastrophe."

Yes, we are what we teach, and that can be magnificent!

Respectfully,
David A. Hancock

# Introduction

*Letters from a Mad Public School Teacher* is intrepid, irascible, cantankerous, provocative, satirical, passionate, thought-provoking, bitingly witty, ironic, sarcastic, iconoclastic, and enhanced with demagoguery.

What is wrong with education? What can be done about it? You just found out. Now you know!

"In years to come, your students may forget what you taught them. But they will always remember how you made them feel."

Also, the following elicited personal and professional reflection:

> As a teacher, I have come to the conclusion that I am the decisive element in the classroom. It is my personal approach that creates the climate. It is my daily mood that makes the weather. As a teacher, I possess tremendous power to make a child's life miserable or joyous. I can be a tool of torture or an instrument of inspiration. I can humiliate or humor, hurt or heal. In all situations, it is my response that decides whether a crisis will be escalated or deescalated and a child humanized or de-humanized. (Haim Ginott)

# American Students Can Hold
# Their Own with the Japanese

Let's set the record straight before we compare Japanese education to American education.

First, we need to understand that the Japanese value harmony, obedience, and conformity ("Youths Ignore Future as the Japanese Worry," Aug. 22). We value pluralism, independence, individualism, and creativity. Japan is a hierarchical society. We favor local control. The Japanese are a homogeneous population. We are heterogeneous.

Statistics show that the Japanese graduate 90 percent from high school compared to our 78 percent. However, more of our students go to college (60 percent to 30 percent). Higher education in Japan is generally conceded to be inferior to that in the United States. The college years are often referred to as a "four-year vacation."

In the United States, students seem to come into their own at the college level. We may not move as fast, but we go further. The first Nobel Prizes were awarded in 1901. Since then, Japan has received only six. When we compare the hundreds of Nobel prizes won by Americans, we have a good index of the positive effects of our educational system. So let's relax on the proficiency test scores.

Also, at the present time, France is experiencing a "brain drain" of talented young entrepreneurs who are feeling the country's bureaucratized hierarchical, anti-innovation culture according to *Global Trends 2005*.

As David Elkind, professor of child development at Tufts University and author of *The Hurried Child* and *All Grown Up and No Place to Go*, states so well, "All our problems in American education arise because we are not sufficiently American, not because we are insufficiently Japanese. Our classrooms are not as individualized, and our curriculums are not as flexible, as our values of individualism and self-reliance demand. True educational reform will only come about when we make our education appropriate to children's individual growth rates and levels of mental development."

David A. Hancock
Chesterland

First letter to editor from Hancock (June 1990) after twenty-one years of teaching!

## Politicians, Money Can't Make Bored Kids Learn

To the editor:

Oh no, not again. More "edu-blather," demagoguery, empty rhetoric, and ad infinitum from politicians, pundits, and "standardistos" about education reform legislation.

Some of the highlights stated were that states would be forced to set annual goals for schools to raise student achievement, would have to achieve proficiency in twelve years, and the worst schools would face staffing overhauls.

First, we can't force an increase in student achievement, just as we can't force humans to increase positive health habits when they choose not to. Second, we can't force proficiency in twelve years. Can we force a cure for certain diseases? Third, how about student overhauls?

I have observed in my thirty-four years as a public school classroom teacher that it's not ADHD (attention deficit hyperactivity disorder) but rather ODD (oppositional defiant disorder) and ICCLA (insouciant couldn't-care-less attitude) from the obstinate cantankerous recalcitrants.

This is something that private / parochial schools do not experience (usually) because if students exhibit behavioral disorders, they are transferred to their neighborhood public school. Remember, private and parochial schools practice first-degree segregation.

To all our critics, let us remember that "no curricular over-haul, no instructional innovation, no change in school organization, no toughening of standards, no rethinking of teacher training or compensation will succeed if students do not come to school interested in and committed to learning," as stated by Laurence Goldberg.

However, it's very difficult if the physical building has any savage inequalities (poor heating, no soap or toilet paper—the appalling Afghanistan cave atmosphere, etc.) or Saddam spider holes.

Before we know it, obstetricians are going to start placing a practice proficiency test in the neonate's crib that will probably cause SIDS (sudden infant death syndrome).

Caution—this is a "no-spin zone" letter from the *H* factor.

David A. Hancock
Chesterland

Hancock is a science teacher at Monticello Middle School.

Public or private, among larger school districts, Cleveland has the highest rate in the state of students enrolled in private schools. An estimated 39 percent of the children living in the district who attend a private school in grades K–5 enrolled in private schools. Here is other Greater Cleveland

Highest Percentage in Private schools

Cleveland Hts.
| | |
|---|---|
| -University Hts. | 39% |
| Westlake | 36% |
| Revere | 32% |
| Mayfield | 28% |
| North Royalton | 25% |

Lowest Percentage in Private Schools

| | |
|---|---|
| Ravenna | 3% |
| Solon | 5% |
| Cloverleaf | 6% |
| Twinsburg | 7% |

# George W. Bush is No "Education" President

To the editor:

So President George W. Bush said that he will be our education president. I didn't think too much about this until I read *Is Our Children Learning? The Case Against GWB* [sic] by Paul Begala.

GWB asked this question on January 11, 2000, in Grand Rapids, Michigan, from "Perspectives" (Newsweek, March 5, 2001): "You teach a child to read, and he or she will be able to pass a literacy test." It's quite evident that you do not need good grammar to be president.

Here are some other enlightening observations: "Higher education is not my priority" (*San Antonio Express-News*, March 22, 1998). "Dubya went to Andover, Yale, and Harvard as a beneficiary of affirmative action for the overprivileged children for the eastern elite aristocracy," according to Begala. As Begala points out, a review of the record reported in the *Fort Worth Star-Telegram* indicates that Texas's most important school reforms took root long before W moved into the governor's mansion. Even Bush aides say that his predecessors (Ann Richards and Mark White, Democrats) are more responsible for improvements in Texas education. It is interesting to note that the University of Texas at Austin turned W down for admission.

As reported, of the top fourteen cities, public schools with more than 50 percent dropout rate are the following: second, El Paso (88 percent); fourth, Dallas, San Antonio (75 percent); sixth, Houston (72 percent); tenth, Austin (60 percent); and thirteenth, Fort Worth (54 percent) (1996 research).

It should also be known that the governor of Texas is not like other governors. She/he has no power aside from signing or vetoing bills and nominating people for state boards and commissions.

The governor doesn't have a cabinet. He doesn't write the budget. The governorship is mainly ceremonial. The lieutenant governor presides over the state senate, chairs the board that writes the budget, and is more powerful than the governor, according to Nicholas Lemann of *The New Yorker*.

As Begala sums up, "The Texas governor can provide a moral example, and Bush loves to give pious, pontification lectures about just how moral he is. One of W's favorite applause lines is that he will 'restore honor and integrity to the Oval Office.'

"When I first heard it, I figured he was referring to the terrible lack of integrity his father showed by lying to the country about his role in the Iran Contra affair. [sic] But then my Bushie friends told me he was referring to the fact that President Bill Clinton had an affair and lied about it. Now, I think having an [sic] affair and lying about it is wrong. But I also think selling deadly missiles to the Ayatollah and lying about it is wrong."

Oh yes, President George W. Bush, our education president. Right. I think I need to take two Extra Strength Tylenol.

David A. Hancock
Chester

# Science Teacher Free to Experiment with Ideas

To the editor:

I appreciate Steven Goden's letter (*The Sun Press*, June 28) that states, "Science teacher fails at logic, open-mindedness [sic]." It definitely stimulated some reflective thinking.

I will simply say that when it comes to political and educational philosophy, I have a penchant to be ostentatious and pedantic. I think there is no direct correlation between political and scientific thinking (except for politics in education.) [sic]

I also think that when it comes to science, I do possess logic, reason, and open-mindedness. Just ask any of my five thousand students whom I have attempted to teach and inspire during the past thirty-three years.

Again, we all have opinions, and I see absolutely nothing wrong with opinionated, biased, demagogic diatribes when it comes to politics, education, and philosophy.

In response to the comment about Texas governors Ann Richards and Mark White, they had a more cooperative legislature as Democrats than George W. Bush when education reforms were passed and implemented, to the best of my knowledge. If I made a gaffe in facts, I stand corrected.

If Goden has any doubts about my professional ethics or teaching, he may come and visit anytime.

David A. Hancock
Chesterland

# Republicans Prove Point

Donald Nichols's "disgusting letter" to the editor responding to David Lange's "disgusting column" reminds me of John Stuart Mill: "Although it is not true that all conservatives are stupid people—it is true that most stupid people are conservative."

I was going to stop with this quote. However, I thought of Maggie Kuhn's quote, "Speak your mind even if your voice shakes."

Donald Nichols and his servile minions should ruminate on the following to elicit some cognitive dissonance, hopefully.

Don't believe everything you think. Question reality. Great spirits have always encountered violent opposition from mediocre minds. Liberals treat dogs like people, while conservatives treat people like dogs. If conservatives are so patriotic, why do they keep sending our jobs overseas?

I think, therefore I don't listen to Rush Limbaugh. Give Bush an inch, and he thinks he's a ruler. Somewhere in Texas, there's a village missing an idiot. Support the troops: impeach Bush. Vote Democratic: The a—— you save may be your own. Eat tainted meat, breathe poison air, drink nasty water, help only yourself: vote Republican. Minimum wage for politicians. Nation of sheep ruled by wolves, owned by pigs. If only closed minds came with closed mouths. The problems we face will not be solved by the minds that created them.

"Everyone seems to be hacking away at the branches of evil while no one is striking at the roots" (Thoreau).

"Great minds discuss ideas, average minds discuss events, small minds discuss people" (Admiral Hyman Rickover).

"Error of opinion may be tolerated, so long as reason is left free to combat it" (Thomas Jefferson).

OK. So what's the panacea to our human relationships? Read and think carefully. Are you ready?

We live in a world of events, and our lives are affected by these events because of the way we see them. This is also true of human beings. People are to us the way we perceive them. Our perceptions are based on qualities that we are not happy with in ourselves— qualities that we use as a means of making a judgment.

As long as you see someone as a problem, you must remain in these circumstances, so you can be right about him or her. It's only when you are willing to allow people to be as they see themselves, without your judgment, that you can free yourself from these circumstances.

Something is missing in today's dialogue of public policy which tends to escape our logic and reason. Maybe humorist P. J. O'Rourke is trying to tell us in his excellent, insightful libertarian book *Parliament of Whores*, "that God is a Republican and Santa Claus is a Democrat. Santa Claus is preferable to God in every way but one: There is no such thing as Santa Claus.

"Democrats are also the party of government activism, the party that says government can make you richer, smarter, taller and get the chickweed out of your lawn. Republicans are the party that says government doesn't work, and then they get elected to prove it."

David A. Hancock
Chester
Republicans Prove Point!

# Stimulating Reproach

After a couple of months of travel-leisure and recreational therapy (retirement is nirvana) as well as a respite and sabbatical from letter writing, it's time to get back to business.

After some catatonic and didactic musings, I need to respond to Thomas Keck's June letter, "Haters of President." I really did get a "Keck" (equivoque intended) out of his perspicacious perceptions. Let's face it—we all talk and write about nouns such as people (small minds); places, things, and events (average minds); and ideas (great minds) in regard to Admiral Rickover's quote "Great minds discuss ideas, average minds discuss events, small minds discuss people."

He then says that he hopes that I do not go off the deep end like my fellow colleague and friend of Patriots for Change, Elliott Berenson. I'll just leave this nonsensical nonsense at that.

Maybe most of us are educated beyond our intelligence. For enlightenment, read any of Howard Gardner's books on intelligence, especially *Five Minds for the Future*.

However, Mr. Keck is on target with "Nepotism at Kenston." I personally observed the "miscreants of the corporate oligarchy" (a.k.a. board of education) choose this behavior several times during my thirty-five-year tenure as a public school teacher.

Kenston School District proves the wit and wisdom of the literary legend Mark Twain when he said, "In the first place, God made idiots. That was for practice. Then he made school boards."

Enough said. Except for this, I've always enjoyed reproachfulness directed toward me since kindergarten. It stimulates my endorphins and neurotransmitters.

David A. Hancock
Chester

# Medicate to Educate

The perceptive and accurate observations by Susanne M. Alexander—Letter to the Editor (PD 5-25-00)—"Why are There so Many Hyperactive Diagnoses?" in reference to overprescribing Ritalin and forcing children into structured, inflexible school environments and crowded day care centers is right on target about finding creative alternatives to medication.

There seems to be a positive correlation among drugs, behavior, and violence in public schools. All the recent instances of school violence has taken place in public schools—not private schools. I wonder why? Very simple: public schools reflect society—private schools reflect selection, segregation in general, and isolation from the real world as well as a very different school climate in terms of student behavior, motivation, attitudes, and academic achievement.

There is an immense difference in what is and what is not tolerated in a public school and what is and what is not tolerated in a private school.

The children who "needed Ritalin" (which disrupts growth hormone production, impairs mental function, and does not improve learning and achievement—just what adolescents need!) in order to control behavior and make them obedient, conforming, and quiet in the public school classroom usually do fine in private school. There is substantial evidence that many classes of psychiatric drugs can cause or exacerbate depression, suicide, paranoia, and violence. Ritalin and the amphetamines (stimulants) are very similar to cocaine in terms of how they affect brain chemistry and function. Eric Harris was taking Luvox (antidepressant prescribed for obsessive-compulsive disorder, which is in the same class as Prozac) at the time he committed ten murders at Columbine High School in Littleton, Colorado, on 4-20-99. It has been recommended that maintaining patience, tolerance, and guidance with children who underachieve is a far more positive action than medicating them.

According to Peter Breggin, psychiatrist, in his books *Toxic Psychiatry* and *Your Drug May Be Your Problem: How and Why to Stop Taking Psychiatric Medications*, many psychiatric drugs often cause the very problems they are supposed to correct. All this talk about biochemical imbalance is pure guesswork. Research in no way bolsters the idea that psychiatric drugs correct imbalances. Psychiatric drugs are spreading an epidemic of permanent brain damage. Someone once asked, "What's the difference between an adult and a child? The adult is on Prozac, and the child is on Ritalin."

David A. Hancock
Chesterland

# Brain Drugs Hazardous

I would like to strongly encourage everyone to read *Warning: Psychiatry Can Be Hazardous to Your Health* by William Glasser, MD, a psychiatrist who has never prescribed a psychotropic drug.

Dr. Glasser, the father of reality therapy, maintains that when we are diagnosed with a mental illness or disorder, such as depression, schizophrenia, bipolar disease, or obsessive-compulsive disorder, and treated with brain drugs, we become one of the millions of geese who lay golden eggs for the multibillion-dollar brain-drug industry. There are big bucks in brain drugs.

"This industry, which masquerades as mental health's best friend, generously funds a variety of groups and activities that promote mental illness and brain drugs. Examples of this funding are lucrative research grants to psychiatrists who can come up with supportive research, plus psychiatric conferences; liberal grants to mental-health associations that vigorously support mental illness and brain drugs; large grants to patient-advocacy groups that do the same; and millions of dollars to fund high-powered public-relations firms to promote the 'new drugs' to cure 'mental illness' and to persuade the media to report these cures.

"The last thing the psychiatric establishment and the drug companies want is for you to get the idea that you can improve your own mental health or help your loved ones to improve theirs at no cost to yourself.

"We are led to believe that if we have psychological problems, we are ill; all we need to get our mental health back is a pill. There is a further price we risk when we take strong brain drugs; many of them harm the brain and cause real mental illness."

As Thomas Szasz, author of *The Myth of Mental Illness*, says, "Giving oneself an addictive drug is a crime; receiving it from a government agent called an 'addiction specialist' is a treatment.

"If a person ingests a drug prohibited by legislators and claims that it makes him feel better, that proves that he is an addict. If he ingests a drug prescribed by psychiatrists and claims that it makes him feel better, that proves that mental illness is a biomedical disease."

David A. Hancock
Chester

# Teachers Can't Educate Kids
# Who Refuse to Learn

To the editor:

Let me save the central office administration some time dreaming up a teacher evaluation form that links teacher instruction to student performance/achievement.

As a public school teacher for the past thirty years, I can say without a doubt that teaching is a hard job (and rewarding) when students make an effort to learn. When they make no effort, it is an impossible one. Despite our hard work, we are confronted daily with increasing numbers of students who are difficult to manage, and even with our best intentions, we are able to do little more than serve as custodians.

However, there is still employment in the United States for the 60 percent who do not learn in school. In fact, low-paying service jobs are proliferating at a much higher rate than high-paying jobs that require an education. Therefore, we are not "a nation at risk" as predicted in 1984.

Let us do the same for doctors that the central office administration of the Cleveland Public Schools wants to do with the teachers and link doctors' pay (evaluation) with the health of the patient (even though the patient has or continues to practice unhealthy behaviors).

Past Superintendent James Penning of the Cleveland Public Schools was right when he said that teachers should not be penalized for factors they cannot control, such as student attendance. What about student motivation and attitudes?

Oh well, I hope that all my students have high intrinsic motivation and good attitudes. If they don't, I can have a sanguine feeling that I am not to blame.

David A. Hancock

Hancock is a nature studies / science teacher at Heights High School.

# Improving Instruction Isn't Enough

In the *Plain Dealer* editorial, "The Quest for the Test" (in reference to Ohio's high school proficiency tests), the following statement was made: "But the testing, and the public humiliation and attention it brings, should be powerful incentives for improving instruction."

It has been my experience during the past twenty-four years that improving instruction does not improve academic achievement just like improving medical school instruction does not improve a person's own health.

Educational reform in terms of outcome-based education works. Many educators have been teaching problem-solving, critical thinking, and cooperative learning for years. We are getting away from memorization (the lowest level of learning) and stressing comprehension, application, analysis, and evaluation.

Learning boils down to what William Glasser, MD, author of *The Quality School*, once said, "We learn 10% of what we read [for the first time], 50% of what we both see and hear, 70% of what is discussed with others, 80% of what we experience personally, and 95% of what we teach to someone else."*

David A. Hancock
Chesterland

---

* This is the main reason why I have my students "play teacher" with their presentations to the class!

Things are more like they are now than they ever were *before*!

# Students Need More Than Miracles

Superintendent Richard Boyd, with a halo of "ivory tower" philosophy, challenged 115 new teachers to educate students without always having the supplies, equipment, and technology. Boyd is sounding like a great majority of superintendents who have not taught living students in a classroom for decades or maybe have never been classroom teachers.

I would love to hear a corporate CEO, hospital administrator, etc., say to his or her staff, "Just do your work, provide quality service and care, etc., without adequate supplies."

Here we go again. When all is said and done, more is said than done, adding excess carbon dioxide to the atmosphere. (Global warming!)

Patricia Smith (the Dick Feagler of the *Boston Globe*) said, "It really does not matter who the superintendent is—it could be Barney the Dinosaur."

What does matter are the attitudes of the human beings inside the school building, support services, and the physical environment.

Boyd also said that kids will give you what you expect. "If you expect little, they are going to give you a little; if you expect a lot, they will give you a lot."

This is somewhat true for the majority. However, in my twenty-seven years of public classroom teaching experience, it has been my observation that there is no teacher, no matter how skilled, who can teach a student who is apathetic, shows indifference, or simply refuses to learn. And we are getting more and more of these students in public school. Then society blames the system for not producing intellectual scholars. We need to remember that we are not dealing with assembly-line, factory-model products. We are dealing with living human beings (even though it may seem like the living dead for some) to develop their minds for the benefit of society. It has been said that when the student is ready, the teacher will appear.

All humans need to remember the famous ten two-letter words: "If it is to be, it is up to me."

David A. Hancock<br>
Chesterland

## Opposite of Progress

Let's keep it laconic! Or should we say *pithy*? In reference to our immigration imbroglio, debacle, or quagmire that seems to be insidious, harrowing, and discombobulating with prevaricating and obfuscating canards, the statement below simply reflects the following:

"What is the opposite of progress? Congress! Welcome to the United States of Mexico." And—"mission accomplished!" As Gary Larson, artist of *The Far Side* cartoon, said, "Adios Amebas." *(Amigos) handwritten note*

David A. Hancock
Chester

# Conflicting Priorities

As is true throughout much of the United States, military recruiters lie to and mislead high school students.

They show up uninvited. They call students at home. They ask personal questions about students' future plans and then assure them that the best way these can be realized is by first joining the military. Want to go to college? Join the military. Want to be whatever? Join the military.

Not surprisingly, recruiters frequent schools serving working-class and low-income communities, usually not wealthy districts.

Anne C. Lewis, national education policy writer, wrote in *Phi Delta Kappan* (March 2006), "The Orwellian Pentagon has a database that contains the names and personal details of 30 million young people—ages 16–23. Parents can write the Pentagon to request that their children's name be removed, but if they do so, the information is moved to a 'suppression' file in the Pentagon's Joint Advertising Market Research and Studies database and is still given to recruiters.

"Several senators and more than 100 privacy groups have requested that the database be eliminated, but the Pentagon officials seem convinced that it is necessary if we are to maintain a volunteer Army. Oh, brother."

Let us recall malingerer Dick Cheney when he said, "I had other priorities than the military."

David A. Hancock
Chesterland

# American Public Schools Dehumanize, Inhibit Kids

To the editor:

Educator John Holt, author of *How Children Learn* and *How Children Fail*, was not an aficionado of either Ritalin or our mass-production school system. Holt told Congress that we give kids this drug so that we can run our schools as we do—like maximum security prisons for the comfort and convenience of the teachers and administrators who work in them.

Holt also inferred that America's public schools are not particularly shining examples of how to bring out the best in young people. Although thousands of humane, caring people work in schools as teachers, aides, counselors, and administrators, a good number of the schools end up teaching little more than obedience and conformity. Research by the Carnegie Council on Adolescent Development concluded, "Many large public schools function as mills that contain and process endless streams of students. Within them are masses of anonymous youth. Such settings virtually guarantee that the intellectual and emotional needs of youth will go unmet."

One of the most penetrating critics of contemporary schooling is New York State 1991 Teacher of the Year, John Taylor Gatto, who states, "The school bell rings, and the students in the middle of writing a poem must close her/his notebook and move to a different cell, . . . it is absurd and anti-life to be part of a system that compels you to sit in confinement with people of exactly the same age and social class . . . it is absurd and anti-life to move from cell to cell at the sound of a loud gong for every day of your youth, in an institution that allows you no privacy."

For the entire school day, students are under surveillance. They hardly have any private time or private space. Many teachers do their best to be humane, but students are typically expected to sit still for hour upon hour and do whatever they are told. This is not only totally unnatural and profoundly frustrating for students, but it also inhibits learning. Human beings are programmed by evolution to develop by moving, touching, and being involved in life's tasks.

Neil Postman said it best: "School and prison are the only two places in the world where time takes precedence over the job to be done. Children enter school as question marks and leave as periods."

David A. Hancock
Chesterland

Hancock is a science teacher at Cleveland Heights High School.

# Letters to the Editor

## SUPERINTENDENT EXCELS

I need to respond to West Geauga Board of Education member Michael Kilroy giving Superintendent Anthony Podojil a grade of C.

I have personally and professionally known Dr. Podojil since 1991 when he became our assistant principal of curriculum and instruction at Cleveland Heights High School. I retired after thirty-five years of teaching experience, all in the Cleveland Heights-University Heights City School District, in 2003. I have had experience with scores of school administrators, including ten superintendents.

I would like to distinguish among grades, evaluation, and assessment. An assessment and evaluation is more valid and reliable than a grade. In my opinion, Dr. Podojil has earned an A-plus in assessment and evaluation. I base my judgment on the Association for Supervision and Curriculum Development, a professional organization involved with educational leadership.

A research study involved twenty-one responsibilities of effective school administrators and a correlation with student academic achievement. The most important are the following:

— *Situational awareness.* Takes note of details and undercurrents in the running of the school system.
— *Flexibility.* Adapts leadership behavior to the needs of the current situation and is comfortable with dissent.

— *Discipline.* Protects teachers from issues and influences that would detract from their teaching time or focus.
— Monitors the effectiveness of school practices and their impact on student learning.
— Fosters shared beliefs and a sense of community and cooperation.
— Establishes a set of standard operating procedures and routines, resources, financial stability, knowledge of curriculum and instruction, communication, ideals, and beliefs.
— Visibility.
— Has quality contact and interactions with teachers, students, and parents.
— Inspires and leads new and challenging innovations.
— Recognizes and celebrates accomplishments published in local newspapers.

Again, an A-plus is my professional grade to Anthony Podojil.

And the answer is no to the question, are you (am I) a sycophant-milquetoast?

David A. Hancock
Chester

Hancock is currently an adjunct professor of education at Notre Dame College in South Euclid.

# Teachers Teach Kids—Administrators Don't

Mayor Michael R. White has given Barbara Byrd-Bennett a 5 percent raise and a 15 percent bonus for her hard work, dedication, performance, and inspirational leadership. I do not recall White expressing this kind of thinking toward teachers, who get a raise of less than 5 percent and no bonus.

Also, Byrd-Bennett is going to Jerusalem to learn more about educational leadership, funded by the Mandel Foundation. In the meantime, teachers are in classrooms (which administrators are happy they are not) doing their best to manage students and encourage them to learn—even the resistant students who are stressed, frustrated, and have physical and mental health problems.

Classroom teachers really resent administrators—especially superintendents. They have zero impact and influence on me personally in terms of inspirational leadership.

All the demagoguery, diatribes, harangues, incantations, and gibberish about US education are nonsense. So-called leaders, especially politicians, cannot make teachers change or improve. No one can make anyone else change or improve. Only each student can make himself improve or change. We can only support, direct, guide, and encourage. Let us get one thing straight: national standards, threats, coercion, administrators, rules, proficiency tests, state and federal regulations, and politicians do not teach kids. Teachers teach kids.

Our job is to teach the kids we have, not the kids we would like to have. Neil Postman, author of *Teaching as a Subversive Activity* [sic] and *The End of Education: Redefining the Value of School*, said it best:

"Children enter school as question marks and leave as periods."

David A. Hancock
Chesterland

This was written in 1998.

## Byrd-Bennett to Plead Guilty

Barbara Byrd-Bennett, who ran the Chicago Public Schools until she stepped down this past spring amid allegations of corruption, will plead guilty to federal charges that she gave a no-bid $20.5 million contract to a former employer in exchange for future employment and a $250,000 kickback for two relatives. Byrd-Bennett, 66, was charged Thursday with 15 counts of mail fraud and five counts of wire fraud. Also facing federal charges are Gary Solomon, 47, and Thomas Vranas, 34, co-owners of SUPES Academy, a for-profit company that trains principals and administrators. Byrd-Bennett, who headed the Cleveland schools from 1998 to 2006, took over the Chicago schools in October 2012. (The *Cleveland Plain Dealer*)

# Schools Become Prisons, but Learning Not Priority

To the editor:

Pedro Noguera, of Rethinking Schools in Milwaukee, makes several valid and thought-provoking points in regard to school violence.

Combating violence is difficult because it is promoted and legitimized by the mass media and by political leaders. While it is difficult to determine to what extent the glorification of violence in movies and on TV affects young people, psychological studies suggest that such exposure has a numbing effect on viewers.

Given the regularity with which violence is used for legitimate purposes, it is not surprising that children are confused about the appropriateness of responding violently to conflicts with others.

Most of the recent violence in public schools has been in upper-socioeconomic suburban communities—not in urban communities. Currently, the most fashionable response to school violence is the tendency toward making schools more like prisons. It is ironic that we are using prisons as our models for safety and security even though prisons are generally not safe places.

Further, these measures are undertaken without sufficient thought to the social and psychological consequences that may result from changing the school environment in this way. For too many students, going to school is a demeaning experience. The anonymity of large schools and the irrelevance of much of the curriculum to the experience and aspirations of children cultivates apathy, indifference, and disrespect toward school and the adults who work there. Feelings of hostility and resentment are exacerbated when some adults are just plain mean-spirited when they deal with children, exercising their authority over children in a pernicious and vindictive manner.

Laurence Steinberg, in his book *Beyond the Classroom: Why School Reform Has Failed*, said it best: "No curricular overhaul, no instructional innovation, no change in school organization, no toughening of standards, no rethinking of teacher training, or compensation will succeed if students do not come to school interested in and committed to learning."

David A. Hancock
Chesterland

Hancock teaches science at Heights High School.

# Teachers Shun Public Schools

To the editor:

What's wrong with this picture? Public school administrators and teachers who homeschool or send their children to a private or parochial school.

If these educators value private / parochial schools so much, why don't they work there? I'll tell you why—money and fringe benefits. Salaries are two to three times higher in public schools. This would be similar to a doctor practicing in Hospital X but choosing Hospital Y for medical treatment.

Charles A. Byrne, who represents the Eleventh District on the state board of education, wrote in another publication that State Superintendent Susan Tave Zelman's 20 percent salary increase to $150,000—and a bonus to $180,000 – was well worth it. I wonder if he feels the same way about public school teachers. I have my doubts.

I never could understand why those who are indirectly involved with students are paid more than classroom teachers, who are. Don't athletes earn more than coaches?

David A. Hancock
Chesterland

Hancock is a science teacher at Heights High School.

# A Last Word on Reform? Don't Bet on It

What terms and phrases come to mind when we ponder education reform? In my thirty years of classroom teaching experience, here are some possibilities: stonewalling, filibustering, phony facades, incantations, pompous ostentations, consternations, debacles, nihilism, arcane jargon, harangues, diatribes, demagoguery, gibberish, and conjurations. It translates to, "When all is said and done—more was said than done!" We still have the assembly-line, factory-model organizational structure—rushed fifty-minute periods and five-minute breaks, seven times a day. No wonder a great majority of students don't equate school with learning. They equate it with stress or purgatory. Some schools have changed to block scheduling, which seems to have helped this psychological dilemma. A colleague said that one of his education professors (you know the "ivory tower" docent academic theorists) said that education will always be a century behind the times. "If we continue to do the same things in the same way and expect different results, then we are indeed insane."

This observation is a product of what Herbert Kohl calls "willed not-learning." In his book *I Won't Learn From You*, Kohl says, "Such not-learning is often and disastrously mistaken for failure to learn or the inability to learn."

"Learning how to not learn is an intellectual and social challenge; sometimes you have to work very hard at it. It consists of an active, often ingenious, willful rejection of even the most compassionate and well-designed teaching. It subverts attempts at remediation as much as it rejects learning in the first place. Over the years, I've come to side with them in their refusal to be molded by a hostile society and have come to look upon not learning as positive and healthy in many situations.

"I came to understand that children in school act in ways that are shaped by the institution; therefore, it is essential never to a judge a child by his or her school behavior."

One final piece of information, as reported in the *American Teacher*, confirms the relative disadvantage of US teachers. The number of teaching hours a year is 958 at the primary level, 964 at lower secondary, and 942 for upper secondary. The overall means for teachers in the Organization of Economic Countries and Development's twenty-three member nations at the three levels are 791 hours, 700 hours, and 630 hours, respectively. This proves the ultimate paradox of more is less and less is more.

David A. Hancock<br>Cleveland Heights

Hancock teaches at Cleveland Heights High School.

# Can't Predict Success

The following is a letter regarding "Math Scores on the SAT Hit Highest Mark in 30 Years" (Aug. 30):

Don't get too excited. An increase of three points means that students are answering two or three more questions correctly.

In my thirty-two years of classroom teaching experience, I still have many students who have taken algebra and geometry fail the ninth-grade math proficiency test. Most lack basic skills with fractions, decimals, percentages, and analytical problem-solving. Let us remember that the SAT is an aptitude test (readiness, ability, talent, knack, skill, proficiency), not an achievement test (success, attainment, triumph, accomplishment). Standardized tests ignore skills and abilities needed to function in a complex, pluralistic society—such as the ability to work collectively in various social and cultural contexts, to adjust to change, to understand the perspectives of others, to persevere, to motivate, to solve problems in a real-life context, to lead, and to value moral integrity and social commitment.

I have known many students who attended prestigious colleges yet have not been "successful" and many who have attended local community colleges and universities and succeeded very well.

As Marian Wright Edelman said, "You can get all As and still flunk life."

David A. Hancock
Chesterland

## Letters

## Homework's Problem

I read with interest the article "Homework Overload—Are We Trying Too Hard?" (Feb. 14). As a public school educator for thirty years, I agree with William Glasser, MD, author of *The Quality School*, *Schools without Failure*, and several other books. As difficult as it may be for both educators and parents to accept, mandatory homework may be the main reason that so many students take schoolwork out of their quality worlds.

Leadership guru W. Edward Deming would say that if 80 percent of the workers will not do what they are asked to do, it is the fault of the system. This is a significant statistic proving that the "do what we tell you to do whether it is satisfying or not," boss-managed system does not work, yet we continue to pay little attention to the system itself.

The way to solve the problem of students not doing homework is exactly the opposite of what we do now: reduce compulsory homework drastically and emphasize the importance of classwork.

David A. Hancock
Chester Township

Hancock teaches at Cleveland Heights High School.

# The Book That Ignited the Great Homework Debate: *The End of Homework: How Homework Disrupts Families, Overburdens Children, and Limits Learning*

Etta Kralovec and John Buell are educators who dared to challenge one of the most widely accepted practices in American schools. Their provocative argument—first published in their book and featured in *Time* and *Newsweek*, in numerous women's magazines, and on national radio and network television broadcasts—was the first to openly challenge the gospel of "the more homework, the better."

Consider the following:

- ☐ In 1901, homework was legally banned in parts of the US. There are no studies showing that assigning homework before junior high school improves academic achievement.
- ☐ Increasingly, students and their parents are told that homework must take precedence over music lessons, religious education, and family and community activities. As the homework load increases (and studies show it is increasing) these family priorities are neglected.
- ☐ Homework is a great discriminator, effectively allowing students whose families have more to surge ahead of their classmates who may have less.

☐ Backpacks are literally bone-crushing, sometimes weighing as much as the child. Isn't it obvious we're overburdening our kids?

"Is it possible that homework isn't good for kids? Dare we even consider such a shocking idea? Does it make children, teachers, and parents angry at each other rather than allied with each other?" (Deborah Meier, author of *The Power of Their Ideas* and *Will Standards Save Public Education?*).

"The increasing amount of homework may not be helping students to learn more; indeed, it often undermines the students' health, the development of personal interests, and the quality of family life" (Theodore R. Sizer and Nancy Faust Sizer, authors of *The Students Are Watching*).

Etta Kralovec, a recent Fulbright Fellow, earned her EdD from Teachers College, Columbia University. She was a high school teacher for over twelve years and professor of education and director of teacher education at the College of the Atlantic for eleven years.

John Buell, PhD, University of Massachusetts, author of *Democracy by Other Means* and *Sustainable Democracy*, has taught at the College of the Atlantic.

Alfie Kohn's *The Homework Myth: Why Our Kids are Getting Too Much of a Bad Thing*.

David A. Hancock
Chesterland

39

## LETTERS

## TEACHERS' BOYCOTTS MIGHT END PROFICIENCY TESTING

To the editor:

Oh no! It's that time of year again—proficiency tests and school district report cards. I would think that by now, most everyone would realize that using an assortment of bribes and threats to try to coerce everyone into concentrating on test results does not work with high-stakes testing. It has been described as educational malpractice by Alfie Kohn in his book, *The Case against Standardized Testing: Raising the Scores, Ruining the Schools.*

In grade 4, of the 97 reported Ohio school districts, the failure rate is as follows: 61 percent, citizenship; 91 percent, math; 72 percent, reading; 14 percent, writing; and 88 percent, science. Thus, it seems difficult to justify holding a fourth-grade teacher accountable for his or her student's test scores when those scores reflect all that has happened to the children before they arrived in class.

So what is the solution to this gargantuan quagmire? Boycotts and civil disobedience, which lead to striking results. Elementary school achievement is high in Japan, partly because teachers are free from the pressure to teach to standardized tests because teachers collectively refused to administer them. For many years, they have prevented the government from doing to their children what our government is doing to our children.

Similarly, teachers in England and Wales stopped the new national testing program in its tracks, at least for a while, by a similar act of civil disobedience. What began as an unfocused mish-mash of voices became a united boycott involving teacher unions, a large number of governing bodies, and mass parental support, according to Kohn. Teachers made it clear that their action was taken on behalf of students, based on their understanding that to teach well for the tests was, in effect, to teach badly.

In Massachusetts, some tenured teachers are "just saying no" to administering the MCAS (Massachusetts Comprehensive Assessment System) without harsh repercussions. However, some teachers received a two-week suspension without pay and a letter of reprimand yet still have their tenured teaching position. The time might be right to "just say no."

David A. Hancock
Chesterland

# Education Spending on Decline

To the editor:

Mark Twain said that there are three kinds of lies—lies, damned lies, and statistics. However, here are some statistics that don't lie.

One-third of our nation's students go to schools that are substandard and environmentally unsafe. Across the United States, state spending on education is being squeezed as the money spent on prisons and corrections expands: education, $27 billion in 1980; $16 billion in 1995 on corrections.

It's been said that it takes a village to raise a child. It also takes a village to abandon a child.

Carl Sagan said it best in his book *The Demon-Haunted World*: "All across America, school bond issues are regularly voted down. No one suggests that property taxes be used to provide for military budgets, or for agriculture subsidies, or for cleaning up toxic wastes. Why just education? Why not support it from general taxes on the local and state levels?"

David A. Hancock
Chesterland

# Blame Students, Not Teachers, for Low Scores

To the editor:

Oh yes—tests, tests, tests. Where is it said that everything worth learning is on a test? The Science Proficiency Test contains 46 questions: 17 earth science (sixth grade in our district); 13 life science (seventh grade); and 16 physical science (eighth grade).

As we are all aware, March was proficiency test week in Ohio public school districts—writing, reading, math, citizenship, and science.

I teach (instruct) eighth-grade physical science at Monticello Middle School in the Cleveland Heights-University Heights School District. I feel really great because if I personally get the blame for any of my students not passing the science proficiency test, I will not feel guilty.

However, I will take 100 percent responsibility/accountability for the sixteen physical science test questions. I feel confident that I covered the basic concepts. However, I'm not very confident that more than 60 percent passed the science proficiency test. We will find out soon.

I reviewed my students' CAT (California Achievement Test) science test scores taken in October. The medium national percentile was 49. Some 51 percent of students scored higher, and 48 percent of the students scored lower.

I'm going to try to find out how many of the proficiency physical science test questions my students answered correctly. My awareness from past proficiency science tests is that students do not need to know any memorized facts. They are usually given in the questions. What students do need to be able to do is read, comprehend, analyze data, draw inferences and conclusions, etc. Students need to learn to read in order to read to learn.

So parents, pundits, demagogues, politicians, ivory-tower idealists, philosophers, and school administrators should not blame teachers if students do not pass proficiency tests. They should put the blame and responsibility where it really belongs—with the students.

I would not blame my dentist if I didn't brush and floss my teeth and developed cavities and periodontal disease.

David A. Hancock
Chesterland

SAT measures your aptitude.

SAT, the Scholastic Aptitude Test, is not an assessment or achievement test. Aptitude refers to "natural ability in a given area," "gift," "knack," "know-how," "talent," "skillfulness," and "capacity for learning." As Marian Wright Edelman said, "You can get all As and still flunk life."

David A. Hancock
Chester Township

The *Plain Dealer*

# Tests That Fail Schools and Students

In schools around the nation, assessment is dominated by proficiency, standardized, multiple-choice (or guess), norm-referenced tests. When high stakes have been attached to these tests—from reporting school scores in the newspapers to making decisions about graduation—teachers are told, in effect, that they should focus on them. As a result, the weight of standardized testing distorts curriculum, instruction, and classroom assessment practices.

Multiple-choice questions treat learning as the memorization of isolated pieces of information, rules, and procedures. This is the lowest level of learning, and this approach assumes that first one learns the bits and only later thinks. However, research has shown that students learn best by thinking and doing. Focusing on the bits provides a weak vision of the content of any field of learning.

Norm-referenced tests place test takers on the "normal" or bell-shaped curve. But how much and what humans know does not necessarily fit such a curve, especially after good instruction. These tests are constructed so that half the students must be below average. Just think—half of all doctors graduated in the lower half of their class. The curve promotes the false belief that many students can't learn very much, thereby reinforcing tracking! Norm-referenced tests also cannot tell us whether students have learned much or not—they are compared only with one another.

Unfortunately, schools at which students historically have scored low on standardized tests—often schools with many students from low-income families, students of color, or students whose first language is not English—are most likely to focus on raising test scores. As a result, these students get a low-level education focused on coaching for narrow tests. They are bored, turned off by school (which seems like purgatory), and don't learn much. The tests are almost useless to teachers, and they provide almost no real information to the public.

David A. Hancock
Cleveland Heights

Hancock is a nature studies teacher at Heights High School.

# Testing for Humanity

The ranking of school districts' academic report cards is an abject, egregious behemoth, which focuses on proficiency test scores and is not the apotheosis of education or learning. It's a cavil policy developed by the miscreants of the corporate oligarchy, the state board of education.

Other publications have advocated "firing principals and teachers—a demolition tactic—cleaning house." Really?

It's a fact that if all the teachers and principals from Solon High School (No. 1) or Chagrin Falls High School (No. 2) were transferred to a similar-sized high school in Cleveland for one year, academic achievement and proficiency test scores would not improve significantly. However, if all the students from a similar-sized high school in Cleveland were transferred to Solon High School or Chagrin Falls High School, academic achievement and/or proficiency test scores may improve slightly. The same analogy applies to elementary and middle schools.

How about exchanging homes for one year? Psychologists and sociologists would really be interested in this paradigm research investigation.

Teachers cannot make students learn and achieve or parents parent. Stop the blaming and complaining now. The most famous ten two-letter words are: "If it is to be, it is up to me." As Mark Twain said, "Common sense is not so common."

The epilogue of *Teacher and Child* by Dr. Haim G. Ginott states, "Dear colleagues: I am a survivor of a concentration camp. My eyes saw what no person should witness. Gas chambers built by learned engineers, children poisoned by educated physicians, infants killed by trained nurses, women and babies shot and burned by high school and college graduates. So, I am suspicious of education. My request is: Help your students become human. Your efforts must never produce learned monsters, skilled psychopaths, educated Eichmanns.

"Reading, writing, arithmetic are important only if they serve to make our children more humane."

"You can get all As and still flunk life" (Marian Wright Edelman).

"The worst sin? The mutilation of a child's spirit" (Erik Erikson).

David A. Hancock
Chesterland

# If We Had Proficiencies in Phys-Ed, Youth Will Fail

To the editor:

This letter is regarding all the demagoguery, hysteria, nonsensical nonsense, and empty rhetoric from the standardistos (noneducators, i.e., politicians).

They know nothing about teaching and learning in a classroom or about the failure rate on proficiency tests—Ohio seniors: math, 46 percent; science, 42 percent; citizenship, 38 percent; reading, 31 percent; and writing, 18 percent—or that 60 percent is the minimum state performance standard to pass. (A 75 percent is needed to pass in grades 4, 6, and 9.)

Doesn't this seem like lowering standards during the senior year? A study has shown that 47 percent of seniors took a science course and 60 percent took a math course in their senior year.

The United States spends $423 million on proficiency-standardized testing. The only state that doesn't administer these tests (zero dollars) is Iowa, even though many states administer the Iowa Test of Basic Skills. How's that for a paradoxical paradox?

This high failure rate could be a direct result of the very poor physical and general health condition of 60-plus percent of our students. After 33 years as a classroom teacher in health education / science, I believe we would have a 75 percent plus failure rate if we had a health / physical condition proficiency test.

Why? I observe many students eating donuts and Doritos at around 8 a.m.; exhibiting symptoms of chronic fatigue syndrome during school hours; plopping their heads down on their desks; eating pizza, french fries, and ice cream for lunch; and walking very slowly and struggling to go up stairs.

They are too lazy to get up and walk from point X to Y in the classroom. ("Mr. Hancock, would you please bring me a pencil?") They sit during physical education class; go to the nurse the period before PE to fake an illness; exhibit effects of alcohol, tobacco and/or drug use, sleep deprivation, obesity; and intentionally fail PE during the regular school year in order to participate during summer school for credit.

Many do not want to dress or get wet (swimming avoidance). I see unplanned pregnancy because 90 percent of students do not know when conception can occur. (I correct this factual error during the first day of class.)

Illinois is the only state that requires daily PE classes of all students K–12. Our children are the most obese of any society in the world, and after smoking, physical inactivity is the single largest health risk factor. Obesity-related diseases cost the US economy more than $100 billion per year. Statistics show that 25 percent of students, grades 4–12, attend no PE classes at all during the school week.

The superintendent of Atlanta Public Schools, Benjamin O. Canada, defends the elimination of recess because "we are intent on improving academic performance and you don't do that by having kids hanging on monkey bars."

The ancient ideal of a sound mind in a sound body was rooted in the view that the truly educated person has learned to manage his/her life physically, mentally, and morally. Training and maintaining the body is part of getting one's overall self into shape. It molds good habits and attitudes and helps discipline the intellect.

Parents should remember to ask their children what they do during recess and PE when they discuss his/her day at school. Better yet, assign homework (just in case the PE teacher didn't) and go for a brisk walk or bike ride. Let's get moving.

David Hancock
Chesterland

Hancock is a science teacher at Monticello Middle School in Cleveland Heights. He was a longtime teacher at Heights High School.

# LETTERS

## COMPUTERS IN CLASSROOM NOT ANSWER TO EDUCATION

To the editor:

This fixation with computers in the classroom is a cheap and quick fix. The problem is, it's not a fix at all, states David Shenk in his book *Data Smog: Surviving the Information Glut.* Shenk calls putting a computer in every classroom like putting an electric power plant in every home. Planned computer obsolescence reaps billions of dollars every year for programmers, manufacturers, marketers, and PR professionals.

To those who don't have a vested interest in coming up with an instant solution to our educational challenges or selling a lot of computer equipment, computers in the classroom do not look like such a terrific idea.

"Perhaps the saddest occasion for me is to be taken to a computerized classroom and be shown children joyfully using computers," Alan Kay, one of the legendary pioneers of personal computing, testified to Congress in 1995. They are happy, teachers are happy, the administrators are happy, and the parents are happy.

Yet in most classrooms, on closer examination, Kay said, "The children are doing nothing interesting or growth-inducing at all."

"I used to think that technology could help students," Steve Jobs said in 1996. "I've probably spearheaded giving away more computer equipment to schools than anybody else on the planet. But, I've had to come to the inevitable conclusion that the problem is not one that technology can hope to solve. You're not going to solve the problem by putting all knowledge onto CD-ROMs. Lincoln did not have a Website at the log cabin where his parents home-schooled him, and he turned out pretty interesting. Historical precedent shows that we can turn out amazing human beings without technology. Precedent also shows that we can turn out very uninteresting human beings with technology."

David A. Hancock
Chesterland

# Even Einstein Couldn't Fix State Science Test Woes

To the editor:

As a science educator for thirty-one years, I couldn't help but muse about the latest proficiency test results, especially in science. Only 25 out of 97 school districts listed passed the fourth-grade science proficiency test, and only 9 of the 97 districts passed the sixth-grade science proficiency test. All seven districts with a 26–27 rating failed the sixth-grade science proficiency test.

I think that the inexorable quagmire created by the Ohio State Board of Education-Teacher Certification Division might have much to do with this. Most elementary teachers with K–8 certification do not have a solid background in science. Most of these teachers had only one or two classes in science. This reflects that just 3 percent of those who are teaching in grades 1–4 and whose duties include teaching science actually majored or minored in science or science education at the undergraduate level. The figure is 30 percent for teachers in grades 5–8.

Few elementary teachers say they think they are "very well qualified" to teach science. It's no wonder that science often gets less time and attention than other subjects.

It is hard to imagine that a teacher who majored in science and who is certified for grades 7–12 cannot teach sixth-grade science, but that a teacher certified for K–8 with one or two science classes can.

According to present Ohio teacher certification standards and requirements, Einstein would not be able to teach physics in Ohio public school classrooms. But he could teach in any private school.

This whole proficiency test conundrum reflects what Mark Twain once said: "There are three kinds of lies—lies, damned lies, and statistics."

David A. Hancock
Chesterland

# Public Schools Mission: Serve All, Not Chosen Few

To the editor:

I must respond to Michael Murray's letter (*The Sun Press*, Aug. 14) that states, "CH-UH spends so much because it's a monopoly." Schools cannot compete for students in the same way that businesses compete for customers. Vouchers do not mean much to a poor child whose parents are given a tax credit of $1,000 to attend a private school that charges $20,000-plus in tuition.

As the late Al Shanker, president of the American Federation of Teachers, said so well, "A real test would be to have volunteers from the non-public schools to take over a number of classes from public schools. Take them as they are—without picking the students they want, or those whose parents are motivated, or those who can afford to pay, and put them under private auspices for a year or two. Then we'll see if the non-public schools have some magical ingredient for their success, and if they do, whether they'll share it with the rest of us."

Meryl Schwartz, president of United Parents' Association of New York City, stated the issue well: "Public school doors are opened to every child—rich, poor, handicapped, gifted. They are the backbone of our American heritage, composed of all races, creeds, religions."

Private and parochial schools (which comprise more than 90 percent of all private schools) cannot and do not make that claim, nor do they have to. Their doors can close on any child. Every parent has the right to choose religions or private education for their child—but not the right to use public tax money to subsidize a private choice because she/he opts not to use available public school services.

The Milwaukee voucher program has allowed a small number of poor parents to send their children to private schools, but it has failed to deliver the educational benefits supporters claimed for it. The most important lesson to be learned from Milwaukee's experiment is not educational but political. It's a lesson in how the white power structure has used the Milwaukee program to advance an agenda that has little, if anything, to do with the needs of impoverished children.

Let's put it this way—when we talk about doctors and patients, teachers and students, lawyers and clients, when it comes down to evaluating results, you can't measure the effects of what we do. Why not? They're intangible. Oh? Why should I pay you for intangible results? Because I've been trained and licensed to practice. Hmmmm . . . all right. Here's your money. Where? I don't see it. Of course not. It's intangible!

David A. Hancock
Chesterland

# Sports Fans Pay, Taxpayers Don't

To the editor:

Regarding Mary Jane Skala's Reflections column (*The Sun Press*, Sept. 16), she stated, "Rothschild said aloud what many taxpayers believe. Higher taxes aside, many voters will fight the levy because they don't' believe they're getting their money's worth out of our schools."

Sports fans have no problem spending $200 plus for attending an Indians or Browns game but complain and vote *no* for a public school levy that costs them $350 a year on average. Question: Are the fans getting their money's worth? All they are doing is adding to the athletes' egregious bank accounts.

It has been proposed that one should go to infant school in France, preschool in Italy, primary school in Japan, secondary school in Germany, and college in the United States.

David A. Hancock
Chesterland

The writer is a science teacher at Heights High School.

## Bus Parents Too

James P. Orr of Cincinnati, quoted in the *Cincinnati Enquirer*, said it well: "Busing children all over town to supposedly create racial balance has virtually done away with the traditional neighborhood-school concept. Now, the 'in' [sic] thing is to bash the parents of these children for not participating in the activities of their children's 'community' schools.

"Would the people who dreamed up busing please come forward with a transportation plan for the parents?"

David A. Hancock
Chesterland

# Letters to the Editor

## SCHOOLS REFLECT SOCIETY

The best known of the blame-the-school documents is *A Nation at Risk*, from 1983, and it serves as an exemplar of the genre. That inane booklet listed fourteen indicators of education decline, thirteen directly related to test scores. The other one was indirectly related to test scores—the complaints from business and industry about the great sums they have to spend on remedial training.

These indicators proved, the authors wrote, that we must dedicate ourselves to the reform of our educational system. Yeah, right!

The schools bore the brunt of criticism over the years of a small variation in test-score decline. However, test scores started increasing, reaching record high levels by 1990. Did the schools get credit for the turnaround?

No! The peak tests scores went totally unnoticed.

This is common. Schools were blamed for letting the Russians get into space first when the USSR launched Sputnik I in 1957. No one mentioned the schools in 1969 when the US put humans on the moon and got them back safely. Russian rockets never managed to even get to the moon.

*A Nation at Risk* blamed schools for our apparent lack of global competitiveness. A decade later, when headlines such as "The US

Economy Back on Top" started appearing in newspapers, no one credited the schools. Many said, "Our schools are failing."

Just in case you forgot some history, let's consider test-score declines in context. The decade of 1965–75 opened with the Watts riots in Los Angeles, which were followed by urban violence all over the nation. The free-speech movement exploded onto the streets of Berkeley, California, barely one year after the assassination of John F. Kennedy.

This was the decade that gave rise to the aphorism, "If you remember the '60s, you weren't there." It was the time of acid rock, Woodstock and Altamont, the Summer of Love, the Beatles, the Stones, Jefferson Airplane, and *The Electric Kool-Aid Acid Test*. In 1965 came Timothy Leary's book and slogan *Turn On, Tune In, Drop Out*. Not exactly a mantra designed to produce high test scores.

It was a decade when 58,000 Americans lost their lives in Vietnam while Country Joe and the Fish sang, "Ain't no time to wonder why, whoopee, we're all going to die." It witnessed the Kent State and Jackson State shootings, the Chicago police riot, Watergate, and the assassinations of Robert F. Kennedy, Martin Luther King Jr., and Malcolm X.

All of which is an extended way to point out, once again, that schools don't exist in a vacuum. Everyone knows this, but many forget it when they start thinking about global competitiveness or the information society or the test scores of other nations.

The principle of data-smog interpretation is "Beware of simple explanations of complex phenomena." This principle might be considered a corollary of a law formulated some seventy years ago by H. L. Mencken: "For every complex problem there is an answer that is clear, simple and wrong."

My thirty-eight years of teaching experience makes me conclude that schools reflect society; society does not reflect schools.

David A. Hancock
Chester

# Write on Preschool Levies

As a proud real estate–tax paying resident and citizen of our community for thirty-five years, I was ruminating and lamenting about our No-No-No voters who chose and decided not to financially support our excellent public school system. Leave no child behind—right!

We are leaving many children behind in my opinion. Oh yes, the war on children is going well in our community, which I'll call "educational terrorism."

It appears that the *no* voters are a morose coterie of avarice, pecuniary, parsimonious mercenaries in their attitude in regard to school finance and funding. Obviously, the panacea would be to rescind the quagmire debacle of Ohio HB920.

We do not want Saddam–spider hole school facilities for our children to try and learn in, do we? We need a safe home away from home for our children with adequate equipment, supplies, well-compensated professional educators, etc., in order to educate our children for a diverse world.

An average of $0.32/day? Big deal! I'm sure many of us spend much more on Starbucks (overrated, phony-facade elitism), alcohol, tobacco, junk food, music, sporting events, entertainment, ad infinitum, ad nauseam. Are we getting our money's worth? I doubt it!

Believe me, we are getting our money's worth and more in terms of our children's education.

Are we getting our money's worth from doctors, lawyers, hospitals, politicians, entertainers, athletes? I doubt it. We are just adding megabucks to their egregious bank accounts.

Remember, if you are not satisfied here, then move to Vegas, Bainbridge, Beachwood, Chagrin Falls, Shaker Heights, etc., and take your child with you. Better yet, go to infant school in France, preschool in Italy, primary school in Japan, secondary school in Germany, and college in the United States.

Let us remember the wit and wisdom of the literary legend Mark Twain: "The greatness of the Nation lies in our Public Schools." And don't forget the homeschooling option of isolation.

David A. Hancock
Chesterland

# Write On

Editor:

Intolerant and antagonistic are two words to describe Mr. David Hancock's 4/18 editorial.

Besides being intolerant to any voter who would dare to vote *no* on a school levy, he makes an antagonistic remark toward homeschoolers. He mistakenly labels homeschooling an option of isolation.

I wonder if Mr. Hancock is aware that most education took place in American homes with either the parents or a tutor (usually a pastor) providing instruction from the time of the Pilgrims in 1620 into the late 1800s.

Those early Americans were such educational extremists! They actually had the gall to use the family Bible to help the youngsters learn to read by mastering the letters and phonics of the scriptures being repeatedly read to them. Alexis de Tocqueville in his travels throughout the colonies and frontier found a Bible to be in nearly every household.

Were these people very literate? The success of homeschooling was the ability of the average citizen to read and understand the *Federalist Papers*, which was specifically written for the common man but is very rarely comprehended today—we've come a long way, haven't we?

Would you say Presidents George Washington, Thomas Jefferson, James Madison, John Quincy Adams, or Abraham Lincoln (and others) were isolationists? They were not, but they were homeschooled. All were taught by their father or mother to read.

Ben Franklin (also homeschooled) taught himself so well in science that he was on the cutting edge of many new scientific discoveries. Andrew Carnegie and Thomas Edison were also homeschooled.

John Marshall, soldier, lawyer, diplomat, and also chief justice of the US Supreme Court (by age 45), was homeschooled. Others taught at home were Mark Twain, Agatha Christie, Florence Nightingale, C. S. Lewis, Rembrandt Peale, Claude Monet, etc.

Today, homeschoolers enjoy social action with various age groups through sport clubs (like skiing at Alpine), speech and debate groups, band, etc. Homeschoolers enjoy socialization without bullies, drugs, constantly hearing the F word, and last but not least, they don't have to worry about someone pulling a gun out and shooting.

Another important item to remember is that a homeschool family pays their taxes in full but doesn't utilize the facilities they help finance.

C. Grougan
Chesterland

# Noblest of Professions

Now that I know C. Grougan is Cathy, it all makes sense as an XX chromosome, estrogen-based letter. I am an XY chromosome, testosterone-based letter, usually.

I'm going to stop the homeschooling debate. Ms. Grougan may call me anytime for more enlightening discussions.

I would like to respond to her perceptions about teacher education as a career and not a job.

I have been very fortunate, grateful, and thankful about receiving many cards and letters from several of my twelve thousand students who thanked me for being an inspiring, iconoclastic, heretic teacher. It reminds me of Henry Adams, who said, "A teacher affects eternity: You can never tell where his/her influence stops."

Several former students are doctors, nurses, teachers, professors. I even had a former student for surgery. It wasn't brain surgery. I have had several former students in my college classes. What a joy!

Teaching is the noblest of all professions. There are good and bad teachers, doctors, lawyers, nurses, etc.

The teaching profession may have the perception of being ideal. Listen to Roy Orbison's song "In the Real World." For enlightenment, our egos' greatest disappointment, visit a school all day. Anyone who would like to discuss school, teaching, and education, please call me. I might even invite you to lunch. You may need Zantac, Head On, and Extra Strength Tylenol, though. Or listen to my radio program on WJCU 88.7 FM, *The Diary of a Mad Professor.*

I have had several of my nursing students tell me about their catatonic, unreasonable, robotic schedules that may elicit somnambulism, narcolepsy, and chronic fatigue syndrome. Simply hire more professionals, a panacea for quality care. It should prevent lethal medical mistakes. I'm sure Dr. House would approve.

Since I seem to be developing Broca's aphasia, I would like to end this harangue, diatribe, or pontification with the following: maybe it's my schizoid personality disorder or hypomania from my amygdala acting up or sophistry.

I'm retired—a first-year baby boomer who just loves to listen to the song by the Mamas and the Papas, "Go Where You Wanna Go, Do What You Wanna Do." Time to go to lunch, have a couple margaritas, take a nature walk through the woods on a sunny afternoon (Robert Frost influence), have a cigar, read, take a nap, listen to some music, ride my bike, schedule my next monthly vacation (Connie Francis song influence, v-a-c-a-t-i-o-n every day of the year) trying to discover nirvana. It sure isn't Chesterland.

In conclusion, "I would rather sit on a pumpkin and have it all to myself than be crowded on a velvet cushion" (Thoreau). "All paid jobs absorb and degrade the mind" (Aristotle). "Everything has been figured out except how to live" (Jean-Paul Sarte).

As Gary Larson of *The Far Side* said, "Adios Amebas!" And avoid being a beast of burden and trying to saw sawdust. In order to accomplish this, read *The Joy of Not Working: A Book for the Retired, Unemployed, and Overworked* by Ernie Zelinski. Notice the initials are EZ!

David A. Hancock
Chester

# Write On

## HOMESCHOOLING ADVANTAGES

Editor,

I want to compliment C. Grougan for an insightful response to my "No-No-No" letter to the editor. I was also delighted that I am aware of your historical references.

I would encourage all parents of preschool children to read *The Teenage Liberation Handbook: How to Quit School and Get a Real-Life Education* by Grace Llewellyn, especially if you believe in homeschooling K–5.

Personally, after 38 years and 20,000 students as a public school teacher-educator 7–12 and counselor, I wish more parents would have homeschooled their children! Then I would not have been exposed to more obstinate, cantankerous recalcitrants that elicited Head On headaches!

Some parents do not trust the public schools to help educate their little geniuses. Maybe they are thinking of Winston Churchill ("I am always ready to learn, but I do not always like being taught") or Mark Twain ("I never let schooling interfere with my education") or Margaret Mead ("My grandmother wanted me to have an education, so she kept me out of school.").

I saw a cartoon with two college-admission counselors meeting with a student and reviewing his college application, which was very impressive: high school valedictorian, student council president, captain of every sport your school offered, four undefeated seasons in every sport, prom king, voted most likely to succeed and most popular, perfect attendance record . . . and their caption? "Advantages of the Homeschooled."

In today's diverse culture, I am still convinced that 100 percent academic homeschooling is isolation. However, all parents should be homeschooling their children in morals and other things that enhance their academic and interpersonal intelligence. Summer vacation is the perfect time to enhance learning.

That's one thing that I always enjoyed about teaching. It wasn't a job, it was a career, plus the school calendar of 180 days, which entitled me to 180 days of vacation/year! I receive 91 percent of my top salary for retirement (which started at age 56) plus benefits. Ah! The joy of being a teacher! We deserve it!

And one more thing, I'm happy that my parents did not choose to homeschool me academically. However, they did homeschool me in morals, values, ethics, Eagle Scouts, travel experiences, etc. They believed what Mark Twain said: "The greatness of the nation is in public schools."

In order to gain a full education, students need to be exposed to a variety of viewpoints and educational ideas, not just those of their erudite parents! Case closed! If you are convinced homeschooling is best, check out the following: ActiveParenting.com, Common Sense Parenting at BoysTownPress.org, HomeSchoolingParent.com, *The Hurried Child* by David Elkind, and *Allow Your Children to Fail If You Want Them to Succeed* by Avril Beckford.

Respectfully,
David A. Hancock
Chester resident

## The Plain Dealer: Letter to the Editor

# TOO MANY ADMINISTRATORS AND NOT ENOUGH TEACHERS

I really had to chuckle when I read the editorial, "Grading New Teachers" (PD May 22, 2000). The question asked was, "What do supervisors—principals and superintendents—say about their teaching skills?" It needs to be pointed out that administrators in general do not have many years of classroom experience. During my thirty-two years of classroom teaching experience, I have only known one administrator with more than five years of classroom teaching experience. Most administrators (most will not admit it) who were fortunate enough with connections—and known as the sycophants— could not wait to escape the classroom.

In 1960, classroom teachers made up two-thirds of the full-time staff of American schools. By 1991, classroom teachers barely made up half of the full-time employees of American education; nonteaching staff had risen from 25 percent to 47 percent in three decades. Between 1960 and 1984 (*A Nation at Risk* alarm, remember?), local school districts increased their spending on administration and other nonteaching functions by 107 percent after inflation—a rate almost twice the increase in per pupil instructional expenses. During the same period, the proportion of money spent on teachers' salaries in elementary and secondary education fell from more than 56 percent to less than 41 percent, according to a fact sheet from *Education Digest.*

A remarkable number of people are being added to the payrolls of public education, none of whom have anything to do with teaching students in the regular classroom. They are guidance counselors, curriculum specialists, psychologists, deputy superintendents, assistant / associate superintendents, coordinators, in-service staff, professional development personnel, etc.

The eminent lawyer Gerry Spence refers to these individuals as the "miscreants of the corporate oligarchy." This scenario also infers the pernicious-elitism factor. There are many examples of public school systems that double central administration when the number of students decreases.

I have found it to be very interesting to observe that once these people go from the classroom to administration, they tend to become idealistic bosses with the elitist halo-effect behavior. If we could read their minds, it would be similar to, *God, I'm so happy and grateful that I am not in a classroom trying to manage twenty-five students.* Many just peek in by the door for a few seconds.

Despite all this nonsensical nonsense, education bureaucrats have continued to relentlessly push for increases in the missions of the schools—expansions that would result in further escalation of noninstructional hiring and spending. I have observed this many times during my thirty-two years of classroom teaching experience— certified classroom teachers being appointed to nonclassroom positions. Personally, I think that noncertified personnel (staff assistants) could be placed in these positions. It would definitely save a copious amount of money.

I think Lee Iacocca said it best when he said, "In a perfect world, teachers would be paid the most, and everyone else would be paid less."

David A. Hancock
Chesterland

# It's Up to You

Personal responsibility is out of fashion these days, but in Shaker Heights, it's imperative that African-American students revive it in the district's quest to raise the achievements of its minority population.

Last week, a subcommittee of Project Achieve released a list of sixteen suggestions on how to raise the achievement levels of minority students. It follows on the heels of the controversial article in the *Shakerite*, the student newspaper at Shaker Heights High School, that claimed that African-American students weren't achieving as well as their white counterparts.

Raising the achievement scores will require the district to refine its teaching methods, offer remedial work, and encourage minority students to take more advanced-placement classes. It will require it to encourage minority students to be all they can be.

But it will also require cooperation of the students and their parents. Too many students admit that grades take a back seat to socializing. Too many said they didn't aim for honors classes because those classes were predominantly white. If so, they are only sabotaging themselves.

African-American students have an opportunity to show the district, the city, and the nation just what they can do.

The Shaker schools are excellent. Students are fortunate to be there. Teachers are dedicated. Classrooms are well equipped. All the African-American programs, Black History programs, and other extracurricular events may bolster black pride, but they won't bolster grade-point average. Only students, teachers, parents, and administrators, working together, can do that by taking academics seriously.

David A. Hancock
Chesterland

# Outside "Experts" Know Nothing About Education

To the editor:

It's that time of the year again. Time for all the demagoguery about public school proficiency tests and education standards from the standardistos (media, pundits, politicians, corporate leaders) who are gushing forth from state boards of education.

Most of this nonsense has a lot in common with septic tanks, says Susan Ohanian in her enlightening book *One Size Fits Few: The Folly of Educational Standards.*

Ohanian points out several sanctimonious examples of obfuscations about the invasion of almost-unattainable education expectations and standards.

It's really getting bad in Atlanta were (stuporintendent?) Superintendent of Schools Benjamin O. Canada defends the elimination of recess because "we are intent on improving academic performance. You don't do that by having kids hanging on monkey bars."

Ohanian responds, "This is monkey business. Treating a kindergartener like a robot or Wall Street broker-in-training cannot help."

For us classroom teachers today, standards are pretty low on the list of things that concern and irritate us. Higher-up are squirrely, uncooperative, resistant, passive, apathetic, indifferent, and there are low–self-motivated students and pushy parents. There is also a lack of administrative support, administrative harassment of teachers, and unsatisfactory environmental conditions.

Isn't it about time to tell the standardistos to "sit down and shut up" (sounds like corpulent Governor Christie) shut up? It seems like everybody is supposed to learn everything. The sad part is that when students are taught everything, they don't learn much of anything. But standardistos believe that teachers teach and students learn. However, students don't necessarily learn what teachers teach.

Standardistos don't talk about how boring school is for most students. Most adults probably could not sit quietly and go through the assembly-line, factory-model maze for one day without feeling like one of B. F. Skinner's pigeons. They would probably need Ritalin.

Ohanian asked 108 California teachers, "What do you think of the nation's education standards?" Not one has seen them. Their attitude is the attitude of teachers nationwide. This too will pass. One teacher said in despair, "Why don't they just build jails next to the schools?" Interesting idea. Since 1980, California colleges and universities have downsized eight thousand jobs. The state's prisons have upsized by 112,000 inmates and 26,000 guards; plus, it seems that public schools are becoming part-time orphanages.

Ohanian discusses Louis V. Gerstner. In 1993, he went from being CEO of RJR Nabisco to becoming CEO of IBM. He got a signing bonus of $4,924,596 plus a generous stock package (around $21 million). She states that in his 1994 book *Reinventing Education*, Gerstner blames teachers for not producing an increasing supply of "world-class workers," which he claims IBM needs. But soon after receiving his signing bonus, Gerstner fired 90,000 of IBM's 270,000 employees—the same kind of highly-trained workers he insists the schools aren't producing. Yet his stockholders love him. IBM's market capitalization is up $70 billion, Ohanian writes.

She also notes that while American corporations are sending jobs to foreign climes with low wages, they are demanding the schools save American business from the threat of foreign economies. "Corporate life is rather mindboggling [sic] in its greed," she notes.

Nobody gets rich worrying about children. But the 1996 Congress gave the Pentagon $9 billion more than it requested while cutting $54 billion from child nutrition programs. Fortune 500 businesses and the Pentagon do not have to resort to bake sales or collecting cash register receipts to buy equipment they need.

Ohanian writes that it doesn't matter that standards ignore the needs of children and sell teachers short. Standardistos move ahead with the education-reform plans dreamed up in corporate board rooms and conservative think tanks. The standards apply to all students, regardless of their experiences, capabilities, learning differences, interests, or ambitions.

She concludes, "These standardistos' statements [sic] prove a major tenet of education: If you're sure you know the solution, you are part of the problem."

David A. Hancock
Chesterland

# Students Must Be Responsible

To the editor:

Before we criticize, let's answer two questions:

Is the medical establishment responsible for your health if you misuse or abuse alcohol, tobacco, and drugs (acquiring emphysema, lung cancer, cirrhosis, etc)?

Is the educational establishment responsible for your learning if you avoid studying and participating in the educational process (i.e., failing proficiency tests)?

David A. Hancock
Chesterland

The writer is a teacher at Heights High School.

# Poor Expectations Explain a Lot

To the editor:

Let's settle some nonsense right now.

John Ogbu, a cultural anthropologist, has done a careful study of the origins of human competence in different countries. Each country had easily identified minority members regarded as outcasts. These outcasts were systematically denied full participation in society. After so many years of harsh repression, such outcast minorities learned their lesson. No matter how hard they worked in school, their future opportunity was extremely limited.

Ogbu's point is that the apparent failure of minority students to complete their schooling (e.g., the high school dropout rate for American Indians is more than 90 percent) has been a functional adaption of reality.

As educators, we need to become particularly sensitive to the motivation issue. We can remind parents and teachers that their attitude can become a self-fulfilling prophecy and that no relationship exists among ability, effort, and ethnicity.

David A. Hancock
Chesterland

# Behavior Shows What Kids Learn at Home, Not School

To the editor:

Powell Caesar's "Perspectives" column (*The Sun Press*, Oct. 28, "School District's Best Public Relations Is Its Students") was an exemplary example of a sardonic diatribe and first-degree demagoguery. Students' rudeness, crudeness, profanity, and rowdiness, etc., reflects peer groups much more than school. Believe me, I can say without a doubt that students do not learn these behaviors in our classrooms.

Instead of education personnel telling (encouraging) the students to be on their best behavior (which we do), how about reminding parents to tell their children to be on their best behavior going to and from school (which I'm sure most do). I observe many adults who exhibit the behaviors that Caesar is writing about.

Here we go again, blaming the school for student misbehavior. The school's primary mission and responsibility is education, instruction, and counseling. We all know what the primary responsibilities of the parents are.

I would like to know when the last time was that Caesar was physically in a Cleveland Heights-University Heights school building. Probably not too recently. I invite Caesar to visit Wiley and look around and see firsthand what is going on (Discover Your Schools' Day).

Caesar is jumping to conclusions and being very judgmental in his perceptions about the correlation between school and behavior. It's unfortunate, but studies show that 85 percent of what humans think about is negative.

The biggest problem we face with our students is apathy and indifference as well as the apathy of parents who are too busy making a living, parents who just can't be reached, parents who support the school but the behavior never changes, and parents who refuse to accept the reality that their son or daughter has a problem and blames the school. There is no ABC approach to dealing with human behavior.

David A. Hancock
Chesterland

# Teachers Should Teach, Not Be Social Workers

To the editor:

A letter in another publication by a teacher in the Cleveland Public School District ("Do School Officials Want Teachers to Give Up?"), along with disturbing photographs inside a few schools, reminded me of Jonathan Kozol's book *Savage Inequalities*. We never see this kind of degradation in hospitals, malls, and government buildings, but it seems to be OK to have conditions of squalor in many schools.

Society wants public schools to be all-purpose institutions. Teachers who thought they were hired to teach subject matter are instead asked to be social workers, moms, dads, therapists, cops, nutritionists, public health workers, medical technicians, psychologists, counselors, and perhaps, in the opinion of some students, jailers.

Phillip C. Schlechty, author of *Inventing Better Schools: An Action Plan for Educational Reform*, said it best: "Schools are not welfare agencies, hospitals, juvenile detention centers or psychological treatment centers. They are educational institutions with the singular purpose of ensuring that all children have school work they can and will do and from which they develop the understandings, skills and insights that are considered important to them and to the culture and society in which they will live."

To paraphrase Dick Feagler in a past column, Where does our school's responsibility for your life and education stop and yours (the individuals') begin?

This is ultimately the "great human question."

David A. Hancock
Chesterland

The writer is a nature studies science teacher at Cleveland Heights High School.

# The Brain behind Bush's Speeches Is Not His Own

To the editor:

I hope everyone realizes that 90 percent of George W's speeches come from the brains of his advisers, not his own brain. Also, all his demagoguery about education standards and testing ad infinitum, ad nauseam, doesn't make him an education president. Why? Here are a few quotes from W:

- "Is our children learning?" (from a speech on Jan. 11, 2000, in Grand Rapids, Michigan; quoted in a book of the same title by Paul Begala).
- "Higher education in not my priority [sic]" (*San Antonio Express News*, March 22, 1998).
- "Laura and I sometimes don't realize how bright our children is until we get an objective analysis" (*Meet the Press*, April 15, 2000).

As Begala states in his book, "It is ironic that a guy who was a crummy student and boasts of his anti-intellectual grievances should choose education as his top issue." He went to Andover, Yale, and Harvard with a 550 SAT verbal. This must be OK because Bill Bradley became a senator with an embarrassing 480, and Al Gore flunked out of college and became vice president.

Marian Wright Edelman is correct: "You can get all As and still flunk life."

David A. Hancock
Chesterland

# Students, Not Teachers, Hold
# Key to Learning Process

To the editor:

After reading Susan B. Ketchum's article (*The Sun Press*, Sept. 14, "National Certificates Hard to Earn") about the National Board for Professional Teaching Standards, I couldn't wait to get a pen in hand and start writing.

"About 800 Ohio teachers have earned National Board certification. What does that mean to the average citizen?" It means that those 800 teachers—just one of every 135 teachers in Ohio—have proven they are at the top of their profession (by the way, the US Bureau of Labor Statistics' *Occupational Outlook Handbook 2000* labels teachers, nurses, social workers, and librarians as semiprofessionals), and the students in those classrooms will get a quality education for that year.

Great. What about the other 107,000 Ohio teachers? Does that mean their students do not receive a quality education? What does quality mean? What about the future years of students? For the teachers who choose to attain National Board certification (which seems to be more appealing to younger teachers with less than twenty years experience), I say good for them and congratulations.

Personally, a $2,500 annual stipend for ten years is not enough to externally motivate the overwhelming majority of classroom teachers (especially those with more than twenty years experience). There are just too many hoops to jump through that require an average of 120 hours to complete. Make it $10,000/year, and now you're talking. I may even consider it with thirty-two years of experience. A much better incentive is teachers being able to retire at any age with thirty years of experience with 66 percent of your average highest three-year's salary (e.g. $62,000, 28th year; $64,000, 29th year; and $66,000, 30th, master's degree plus equals $64,000 × 0.66 equals $42,240). However, the State Teachers Retirement System has increased the incentive to 35 years at 87.5 percent. This is much more appealing to teachers with thirty-plus years of experience. National Board certification is not given much thought.

Now think about this. A recent study by the Rand Corporation, a California think tank, of student performance in forty-four states found that higher teacher salaries had "little effect" on outcomes. Similarly, "having a higher percentage of teachers with a master's and doctorates and extensive teaching experience appears to have comparatively little effect on student achievement across states." Stiffer teaching-licensing requirements would, for example, compound the teacher shortage by making it harder for people to switch careers into teaching.

A better approach would be for states to "scrap nearly all the hoops and hurdles that discourage good candidates from becoming teachers," writes Chester Finn of the Thomas B. Fordham Foundation. In his book *Beyond the Classroom: Why School Reform Has Failed and What Parents Need to Do*, Laurence Steinberg states, "No curricular overhaul, no instructional innovation, no change in school organization, no toughening of standards, no rethinking of teacher training or compensation will succeed if students do not come to school interested in and committed to learning. In order to understand how this commitment develops, we need to look not at what goes on inside the classroom, but students' lives outside the school's walls. Until we do this, school reform will continue to be a disappointment and our student achievement will fail to improve."

Personally, I think that I have been at the top of my career in teaching/education for many years—without National Board certification with two master's degrees. I also think I am giving my students a quality science education. However, year after year, I have many students who are apathetic, indifferent, and unprepared to exert effort to achieve academically. I don't think that obtaining National Board certification will help any of my students, while wondering why 100 percent (probably) of students give their best efforts in sports and extracurricular activities and events.

David A. Hancock

# Back-to-School Terror

It's a new school year. Are our parents and students ready? I doubt it!

Oh yes, it's that time of year again. Time for a new academic school year—purgatory for many—to begin. Time for teachers to act as affable paragons, moms, dads, police, nurses, therapists, social workers, and nutritionists as well as teach our subject matter.

In a way, I empathize with students because they are probably thinking, *Oh no! Back to the assembly-line, factory-model prison with seven or eight forty-minute periods, four-minute hall-passage traffic jams, twenty-minute Zantac lunch, rush-hurry syndrome, memorizing, proficiency-test preparation, sitting down, being quiet, lack of enough recess and physical-education time, nonsensical homework overload / overdose, and a perfunctory routine with no air conditioning on hot, humid days.* The school Zeitgeist syndrome?

Nowadays, with the perceived "external, psychological, academic-stress" achievement disorders and to be human robots, Dennis the Menace would be on Ritalin and Charlie Brown on Prozac.

I hope parents did a good job of homeschooling their children, especially character-social skills, for the past eleven weeks.

An example of the "thirteen-year sentence" begins with education malpractice and education terrorism with the school supplies lists. I will use Mayfield public school kindergartens as an example, although most public and parochial schools are very similar, unfortunately.

- Three boxes of Crayola Original Markers—fat ones, basic colors
- One pair of child Fiskars school scissors with rounded ends and metal blades
- Two Expo 2-in-1 Dry Erase Markers—thin, black
- Ten two-pocket folders, no fasteners—two red, two yellow, two green, two blue, two purple
- Ten large Elmer's All Purpose School Glue Sticks
- Ten sharpened pencils
- One fat yellow highlighter
- Two packages of baby wipes
- One family box of tissues (probably for crying)
- One container of Clorox wipes
- One bottle of Elmer's Glue—7.625 ounces
- One large T-shirt that fits over clothing to be used while painting
- One ream of white copy paper (no way)
- One eleven-by-fourteen spiral-bound sketch pad, no lines
- Pair of tennis shoes for physical education (good idea)
- Large, nonrolling backpack to carry belongings to and from school daily (preparing your child for lumbar vertebrae surgery)

I would like to add some essentials that have been overlooked: American flag, cell phone, phone number of child's therapist, calculator, dictionary, thesaurus (English-Spanish).

The shibboleth of "Leave no child behind" has been changed to "Leave no child a dime." For enlightenment, read *The Schools Our Children Deserve* by Alfie Kohn and *Why Schools Fail* by Bruce Goldberg.

David A. Hancock
Chesterland

# It's That Time of Year

Oh yes, it's that time of year again. Time for a new academic school year to begin, time for teachers to act as moms, dads, cops, nurses, therapists, social workers, nutritionists, and affable paragons—which should equal a salary of $100,000!

I'm writing this after I recalled the Staples TV commercial where Dad is smiling and overwhelmed with joy, running around getting school supplies, while Daughter and Son are standing there looking very sad and unhappy.

As a very happy retired public school teacher (thirty-five years), I empathize with Daughter and Son because they are probably thinking, *Oh no! Back to the assembly-line, factory-model prison with six or seven forty-minute classes, five-minute rush-hurry hall passage, twenty-minute lunch (indigestion / Zantac time), memorizing proficiency test preparations, sit-down-be-quiet attitude, lack of physical exercise and personal autonomy, and nonsensical nonsense homework* (which I never assigned). *When do I get to relax from the perfunctory schedule, let alone get a drink of water and visit a restroom?*

It's a paradoxical paradox when we encourage them from birth to two years of age to walk and talk, then all of a sudden, to sit down and be quiet. Humans are not like Skinner's pigeons or Pavlov's dogs. What if Pavlov used a cat?

I hope parents did a good job of homeschooling their children in educational experiences / activities as well as attitude-character and social-interpersonal skills for the past eleven weeks. However, it's been my observation and opinion that over 75 percent of parents would earn a D or F on their report card.

A person said to me recently that "schools are prisons, Saddam spider holes in some cases, and day care centers / warehouses staffed with overpaid babysitters."

This reminded me of a cartoon that said, "Mom, Dad, we are not learning anything in school because we are taking tests."

I suppose it all depends on one's point of view / perception. The college professor said, "What are they doing in the high schools of this nation? This student can't even think." The high school teacher said, "What can you expect? Those middle school teachers just aren't doing their job." The middle school teacher said, "Good grief, those elementary teachers didn't teach this child anything." The elementary teacher said, "What did that kindergarten teacher do? This child isn't prepared for school." The kindergarten teacher said, "This child is impossible. What must his/her parents be like?" And the mother said, "Don't blame me. Have you seen his father's side of the family?"

In all seriousness, let's put the responsibility of personal deportment and academic achievement where it belongs—on our children, with parents' and teachers' leadership and guidance in a safe environment—and hope for the best.

Let us recall the wit and wisdom from the literary legend, Mark Twain.

"Education is what you must acquire without any interference from your schooling."

"Out of the public schools grows the greatness of a nation."

"In the first place God made idiots. That was for practice. Then he made school boards."

David A. Hancock
Chester

# Minority Achievement Must Be Studied Locally

To the editor:

In reference to the black/white achievement gap in schools, the *Harvard Education Letter* has published numerous articles on this subject.

Pedro A. Noguera taught at the University of California, Berkeley Graduate School of Education, and was the leader of the Diversity Project at nearby Berkeley High School. He is now professor of communities and schools at the Harvard Graduate School of Education and has learned some valuable insights: differences in achievement originate outside of school.

They originate in inequities in homes, in socioeconomic status, etc. Nothing new here; schools exacerbate those disparities because they consistently give less to the students who need more and more to the students who have more.

Kids will tell you that when they encounter a good teacher who can inspire them, they become motivated. I have found this to be absolutely true during my thirty-four years of public school teaching experience.

Black students feel less connected to school and believe they have more negative relationships with their peers and their white counterparts.

There's a perception that if you do the same thing, you'll get a worse punishment if you're black.

I have personally observed the following: Black students achieve more academically with both white teachers and black teachers, depending on the teacher's attitude, personality, and behavior. Black students exhibit oppositional defiant disorder with coercive black and white teachers, white students with white and black teachers.

Some teachers' expectations for black students are lower than they are for white students, while lower-performing schools tend to be staffed by teachers who have less experience, fewer advanced degrees, and higher absenteeism. Districts may need to conduct homegrown research on student attitudes, teacher attitude / satisfaction, class size, tracking, etc., before we understand how to change student learning.

It's true that some black students choose to be D students (usually a lack of effort, not ability, motivation, and negative attitude) and project/exhibit their anger toward high-achieving black students and say, "Are you trying to be white, 'N'?" However, more commonly, low-achieving, antiacademic black students simply segregate themselves from their high-achieving peers, both black and white.

Refer to AfricanAmericanImages.com for further information.

David A. Hancock
Chesterland

# Answers Aren't So Good

Questions, questions, questions.

Politician: If schools of education are so good, why are public and charter schools so bad?

Educator: If medical schools are so good, why is there obesity, disease, cancer, diabetes?

If law schools are so good, why is there crime and injustice?

If schools of economics are so good, why is there poverty, greed, and an unstable stock market?

If history departments are so good, why is there war? And why do we learn from history that we never learn anything from history? Or is history just one damn thing after another?

If religious and theology departments are so good, why is there hate and evil?

If political science departments are so good, why are there venal, narcissistic, megalomaniac politicians? Why do they call politics a science?

If schools of dentistry are so good, why is there periodontal disease?

If science departments are so good, why is there global warming and pollution?

Politician: I guess Gertrude Stein was right when she said, "There ain't no answer, there ain't going to be any answer. There never has been an answer. That's the answer."

Educator: Science seems to have a possible answer. In science, it's dangerous to lie. If discovered, the liar is cast out of the group as a faker, fraud, quack, and charlatan. In religion, politics, and psychiatry, it's dangerous to tell the truth. If discovered, the truth teller is cast out of the group as a heretic and traitor. The problems we face will not be solved by the minds that created them. You can get all As and still flunk life. As Mark Twain said, "I never let schooling interfere with my education."

David A. Hancock
Chesterland

# Kids Who Choose Not to Learn
# May Have Right Idea

To the editor:

What terms or phrases come to mind when we think and ponder education reform / restructuring? In my 30 years of classroom teaching experience, here are some possibilities: stonewalling, filibustering, phony facades, incantations, pompous ostentations, consternations, debacles, nihilism, arcane jargon, harangues, diatribes, demagoguery, gibberish and conjurations are just a few that come to mind which translates to "When all is said and done — more was said than done."

We still have the assembly-line factory model organizational structure (hurry-rush 50 minute periods; five minute break; seven times a day) until we feel like one of B.F. Skinner's pigeons. No wonder a great majority of students don't equate school with learning; they equate it with stress or purgatory. Some schools have changed to block-scheduling, which seems to have helped this psychological dilemma. A colleague of mine said one of his education professors (you know, the ivory tower docent academic theorists) said that education will always be a century behind the times: "if we continue to do the same things in the same way and expect different results, then we are indeed insane."

David T. Kearns, chairman and CEO of Xerox Corporation, said, "Public education in this country is in crisis. America's public schools graduate 700,000 functionally illiterate students every year and 700,000 more drop out; four out of five adults in a recent survey couldn't summarize the main point of a newspaper article, or read a bus schedule, or figure their change from a restaurant bill." In his book *I Won't Learn from You*, Kohl goes on to say, "Such not-learning is often and disastrously mistaken for failure to learn or the inability to learn."

"Learning how to not-learn is an intellectual and social challenge. Sometimes you have to work very hard at it. It consists of an active, often ingenious, willful rejection of even the most compassionate and well-designed teaching. It subverts attempts at remediation as much as it rejects learning in the first place. It was through insight into my own not-learning that I began to understand the inner world of students who chose to not-learn what I wanted to teach. Through the years, I've come to side with them in their refusal to be molded by a hostile society and have come to look upon not-learning as positive and healthy in many situations. I came to understand that children in school act in ways that are shaped by the institution; therefore, it is essential never to judge a child by his or her school behavior."

One final piece of information as reported in The American Teacher confirms the relative disadvantage of US teachers. American teachers' workloads are the highest of any OECD (23 member) countries. The number of teaching hours per year is 958 at the primary level, 964 at lower secondary and 942 for upper secondary. The overall means for teachers in the OECD nations at the three levels is 791 hours, 700 hours and 630 hours, respectively. This proves the ultimate paradox of more is less and less is more.

David A. Hancock
Chesterland

Hancock teaches science at Heights High School.

# Teacher Says Many of His Students Learn and Excel

To the editor:

I must respond to Frank. E. Wrenick's letter (*The Sun Press*, Feb. 18, "Nonteaching Teacher is Wasting CH-UH Tax Money"). First, I did not write the headline "Kids Who Choose Not to Learn May Have Right Idea." Second, I quoted Herbert Kohl from his book, *I Won't Learn from You*. There should have been quotation marks around the paragraph that Wrenick is referring to as my personal opinion ("Learning how to not-learn is an intellectual and social challenge . . ."). Student apathy and indifference is at an all-time high by my observations (and many others).

I do promote unguided inquiry and indirect teaching. I manage, counsel, guide, and instruct/teach my students in that order generally. I invite Wrenick to visit our nature / natural history museum classroom anytime. I do not think I am doing a disservice to my students (ask them) or to the citizens of Cleveland Heights and University Heights. I simply manage students without coercion.

I feel very fortunate in receiving many, many letters and cards from former students and parents thanking and praising me for being a positive role model and educational leader. In my thirty years of teaching, I have done my best to practice the words of William Arthur Ward: "The mediocre teacher tells. The good teacher explains. The superior teacher demonstrates. The great teacher inspires." I am doing what I am paid to do—manage, counsel, guide, and teach (inspire).

David A. Hancock
Chesterland

# Leave No Child Behind

The positive connection and correlation between funding and excellence in education is often debated.

However, as reported in the *Review of Education Research* in "The Effect of School Resources on Student Learning and Achievement," a group of researchers from the University of Chicago who analyzed thirty-two studies on this issue concluded that higher per-pupil expenditures; parent involvement and support; more educated and experienced teachers, administrators, and support staff as well as smaller classes, all directly a result of higher funding, are strongly related to improved student learning.

As a resident of Chester since 1972 and with two daughters, 1992 and 1996 West G. graduates, who received an excellent education, I will vote *yes* for our renewal levy—renewing support and confidence with our school system and the education services provided for our children.

It's a fact that our school grades reflect our community grades (i.e., our schools succeed primarily because of the conditions and culture in our community).

All this reminds me of a poster on a bulletin board outside of an office at a local college: "It will be a great day when our public schools get all the money they need, and the air force has to hold a bake sale to buy a bomber."

Let us remember the wit and wisdom of Mark Twain: "The greatness of the nation lies in our public schools."

A *yes* vote means leaving no child behind. Yes, we can continue with "Excellence through tradition and innovation."

David A. Hancock
Chester

# School-Funding Reality

Why is the Cleveland Metropolitan School District having so many financial problems? The answer to this question should be examined from a business approach.

In a business setting—and make no mistakes, that's exactly where a school system is—the bottom line is the main determination of success or failure. In using this approach, the income statement is the first item to be reviewed. The amount of income determines whether a business lives or dies. And further, what is done with that income will also have an impact.

However, the Cleveland School District has very little control over the income it receives. Unfortunately, it is at the mercy of the government bureaucracy, to wit: Gov. John Kasich's lower taxes for the rich (to the detriment of all other budgets); the state legislature, which approved the governor's budget; Cleveland Mayor Frank Jackson; the City Council; and last but not least, the voters who put all the aforementioned into office.

If the Cleveland School District had some control over the income, there might be some reasonable cause to blame them for poor management, but their only action can be a reaction to the financial starvation diet that is denying it the funds necessary to function in a more effective manner. And a fiscal plan is viable only so long as the rules are stable and do not change. Unfortunately, the rules are always changing, and the school district has to deal with the consequences.

Governor Kasich seems to think that the key to balancing the budget for the state of Ohio is to cut services to those programs that need governmental help the most. His Darwinian approach is out of touch with reality. If he were to tax those entities that can afford it, the approach would be more viable rather than watching a necessary public institution fail, condemning that institution, and then, with the voucher program, diverting money to the charter schools.

The mayor and the City Council have also contributed to the reduction of funding for the schools. In order to lure more businesses to Cleveland, the Cleveland City Government has utilized property tax abatements. These abatements have been given to most of the more successful businesses.

The solution to the problem is to find another source of revenue to fund the schools. The property-tax system has already been declared illegal by the Ohio State Supreme Court. For that reason alone, Cleveland should investigate another method for funding the schools. How about an additional 1 percent income tax to be used exclusively for the schools?

This method of funding would be preferable to cutting expenses by gutting the system of any teachers with experience and/or seniority. To be honest, anytime an administrator starts talking about the evils of seniority, the comment is a veiled reference to the elimination of higher-priced professionals by using less experienced, less costly help. Any individual who thinks that this method is in the best interest of the students is not being honest or realistic.

David A. Hancock
Chester

# Look Around: Money Can't Buy Happiness

To the editor:

The Frank Gruttadauria and Enron sagas should remind us of human vultures—parasites at work. It is quite obvious that these individuals have the disease called "more." More money, of course. It reminds me of a few enlightening quotes about economics:

> "The only thing wealth does for some people is to make them worry about losing it." (Antoine de Rivarol)

> "Poor and content is rich and rich enough." (Shakespeare)

> "$1 million doesn't always bring happiness. A person with $10 million is no happier than a person with $9 million." (Unknown)

Ben Franklin expressed the folly in trying to achieve happiness through money: "Money never made a man happy yet nor will it. There is nothing in its nature to produce happiness. The more a man has, the more he wants. Instead of its filling a vacuum, it makes one."

Total security based on external possessions is another illusion of life. The people who are striving for security are among the most insecure, and the people who least care about security are the most secure. Emotionally insecure people seek to offset their unpleasant feelings by accumulating great amounts of money as security against attacks on their egos.

People striving for security, by their very nature, are very insecure. They depend on something outside themselves, such as money, spouses, houses, cars, and prestige or security. If they lose all the things they have, they lose themselves because they lose everything on which their identities are based.

If money makes people happy then why didn't Ivan Boesky, who illegally accumulated more than $100 million through insider trading on Wall Street, stop his illegal actions after accumulating $2 million or $5 million but instead continued accumulating more millions until he got caught (or felt guilty)? Sound familiar?

Why do so many well-paid baseball, football, and basketball players have drug and alcohol and gambling problems? Why do doctors, one of the wealthiest groups of professionals, have one of the highest divorce, suicide, and alcoholism rates of all professionals? Why do the poor give more to charities than the rich? Why do so many rich people get in trouble with the law? Why do so many wealthy people go to see psychiatrists and therapists?

These are just a few warning signs that money doesn't guarantee happiness.

David A. Hancock
Chesterland

Hancock is a science teacher at Monticello Middle School in Cleveland Heights.

# Machiavellian Duplicity

The following morsels are ruminations about West Geauga Board of Education member Michael Kilroy's school-renewal levy campaign ads published in local newspapers. I don't intend to be crass.

First, I think Mr. Kilroy's Smart Board campaign and focus on technology in education reflected positive educational leadership. Also, research on interest rates seems to be positive.

However, I am more concerned about the following attitudes and behavior, ego and power. Many statements reflect some common political demagoguery—e.g., Mr. Kilroy's iconoclasm and intransigent attitude and opinion about the professional positions of superintendent, former business manager, treasurer, and communications director. He seems to think that these positions should be part-time or share them with other school districts. What?

Many of Mr. Kilroy's statements and comments are a reflection of Machiavellian duplicity: disguising of true intentions by deception, deceptive words, or actions. *Obfuscations*—"confusing the issues" or "to make obscure" or "discombobulating." *Prevarications*—"to deviate from the truth" or "equivocate." *Verisimilitudes*—"the quality or state of appearing to be true or real."

*Confabulations*—"fabrications." *Hyperbole*—"exaggerations." *Caviling*—"to make frivolous objections or raise trivial objections." *Captiousness*—"an inclination to find fault, especially in certain people." *Sophistry*—"subtle deceptive reasoning or argument." These are all narcissism traits and characteristics.

Mr. Kilroy has obsessive-compulsive thinking about ranking and test scores. Mark Twain said that "there are three kinds of lies: lies, damn lies and statistics."

Mr. Kilroy would probably conclude that Chagrin Falls schools have higher test scores than West Geauga because Chagrin Falls spends $11,044 per student, while West Geauga spends $10,461 per student.

*Ron Hill's Oct. 29 *Chagrin Valley Times* parody, satire, caricature cartoon in reference to school cuts and *The Texas Chain Saw Massacre* reflects Mr. Kilroy's opinion and attitude in regard to school finance-funding perfectly.

In conclusion, Mr. Kilroy should move to Chagrin Falls and run for the board of education. He would probably be much happier. A sense of pernicious elitism? Change the name of West Geauga School District to Kilroy Pro-Bono Online Smart Board Virtual Academy.

I would also remind Mr. Kilroy that he is a board of education member, not a micromanager or pseudovirtual superintendent.

David A. Hancock
Chester

## Letters to the Editor

# FALLACIES OF NEGOTIATION

Some didactic pensive musings and morsels in reference to faculty (teacher-educators) and boards of education administration (which can be Chagrin), equivoque intended.

Words that describe negotiations: animus, miasma, acrimony, narcissism, megalomania, power, ad hominems, Machiavellian duplicity, and atavistic appeals to indulge in autocratic-dictatorial behaviors.

A recent letter in which a graduate supported giving back to Chagrin Falls teachers reminded me of Henry Adams: "A teacher affects eternity—You can never tell where his/her influence stops."

It seems that teachers do what lawyers do with less pay, harsher judges, and tougher juries.

"The principle of diplomacy-negotiation(s): Give one take twenty" (Mark Twain).

"Conference: A gathering of people who singly can do nothing but together can decide that nothing can be done" (Fred Allen).

"Confirmation bias: I will look at any additional evidence to confirm the opinion to which I have already come" (Lord Molson, British politician).

Reform: "It is essential to the triumph of reform that it should never succeed" (William Hazlitt, English writer).

"If you're going to fight, don't let them talk you into negotiating, but if you are going to negotiate, don't let them talk you into fighting" (A. Lincoln).

"Let us never negotiate out of fear, but let us never fear to negotiate" (John F. Kennedy).

During my thirty-five years as a teacher-educator (1968–2003), all in the Cleveland Heights-University Heights City School District, I observed administrators elicit boss-dictator personality characteristics who preferred servile minions, sycophants, and milquetoast teachers. We know what happens to these individuals (the miscreants of the corporate oligarchy).

When teachers strike, students strike. Oppositional defiant attitudes and behaviors are elicited. Scab substitutes become supervisors in an urgent day care center orphanage.

I experienced three strikes during my professional career: 1978, one-day "wildcat strike" (very effective, unannounced surprise); 1980, two days; and 1982, eight days. Much community pressure was placed and focused on the board of education administration, not the teachers.

Game theory is the study of strategic, interactive decision-making among rational (hopefully) individuals. Anytime people are making decisions that affect others or in response to the actions or even the expected actions of others, they're playing a game.

Recommended readings, research, reflections, and assignments for homework and professional development are the following:

- *Getting to Yes* and *Getting Past No* by William Ury, Fisher-Harvard Negotiation Project.
- *Negotiate to Win* by Jim Hennig.
- *The No Asshole Rule: Building a Civilized Workplace and Surviving One That Isn't* by Robert Sutton.

- "The Toxic Dozen: 12 Rules for Administrators Who Wish to Subvert Teaching," Journal of the American Federation of Teachers: *Changing Education*, Spring 1968.

Hopefully, there is no strike.

David A. Hancock
Chester

# Mysteries of Sexuality

Question: What do the following fallible humans probably have in common? As we know, we are all responsible and accountable for our choices, decisions, and end behaviors. You may or may not recognize some of these names from this sample tryst list: Tiger Woods, Arnold Schwarzenegger, Gen. David Petraeus, Jimmy Dimora, John Edwards, John Ensign, Mark Sanford, David Vitter, Newt Gingrich, Bill Clinton, and Eliot Spitzer.

Possible answer: They are loony lechers and knaves. "I can resist everything except temptation" (Oscar Wilde). "My brain is my second most favorite organ" (Woody Allen). Narcissistic megalomaniacs.

*Are Men Necessary?: When Sexes Collide* by Maureen Dowd.

Analysis: The seminal perspicacious writings of Sigmund Freud in *The Psychopathology of Everyday Life* and *Civilization and Its Discontents* (and malcontents?) are definitely thought-provoking. Dr. Freud frequently makes the point that we are born between urine and feces, except caesarean sections, in reference to the proximity between the sexual and excretory organs.

Perfunctory sex / coitus is an unsatisfying substitute for masturbation.

Thomas Szasz, MD, in *Words to the Wise: A Medical-Philosophical Dictionary*, states, "Traditionally, men used power to gain sex, women, sex to gain power. The new ethic of equality between man and woman must come down to one of two things: either, as the romantics hope, that neither men nor women will use power to gain sex; or, as the realists expect, that both men and women will use power to gain sex, and sex to gain power."

It took men thousands of years to realize that women are human. It takes only a few decades (for women) to discover/realize that men aren't!

Also, the uneasy cycle between the sexes seems to be as follows: "Women always fear the men are going to keep them from getting some advantage because of their sex, and men fear that women are going to get some advantage because of their sex."

Arnold Schwarzenegger, in a magazine interview on his life as a bodybuilder, said, "Having chicks around is the kind of thing that breaks up the intense training. It gives you relief, and then afterward, you go back to the serious stuff."

Conclusion: What would Dr. Freud think? He might agree with C. M. Meston and D. M. Buss in *Why Women Have Sex: Understanding Sexual Motivations from Adventure to Revenge (and Everything in Between)*, which offers an unparalleled exploration of the mysteries underlying women's sexuality. Using women's own words, and backed by extensive scientific evidence, the authors delve into the use of sex as a defensive tactic, as a ploy to boost social status, as a barter for household chores, and even as a cure for a migraine headache.

On the tryst list, the spouse of Luv Gov of South Carolina Mark Sanford divorced him, as well as Tiger Woods's spouse and Arnold Schwarzenegger's; Judge Susan Webber Wright, who wrote in reference to President Clinton's tortured definition of his tryst, said, "It appears the president is asserting that Ms. Lewinsky could be having sex with him while, at the same time, he was not having sex with her."

As John Milton said in *Paradise Lost*, "The mind is its own place and in itself can make a heaven of hell, a hell of heaven." And Zsa Zsa Gabor in the *Observer* said, "Personally, I know nothing about sex, because I've always been married."

David A. Hancock
Chesterland

Additions:

- D. J. Trump
- Bill Cosby

(et al)

- Roger Ailes
- Bill O'Reilly

Pedophiles

# Peace

War. War. War. The US spends $355 billion a year making war. That's $11,000 a second. 1-2-3-4-5. Are we up to your salaries yet?

Of the 22 countries that the US has bombed since the end of WWII—including the long-forgotten raids like Congo (1964), Libya (1986), and Panama (1989)—in how many instances did a democratic government, respectful of human rights, occur as a direct result? None. Iraq will be added to the list.

Maybe we should remember some famous quotes. "In war, whichever side may call itself the victor, there are no winners, but all are losers" (Neville Chamberlain, 1938). "War is the continuation of politics by other means" (Karl Von Clausewitz, 1832).

"Laws are silent in time of war" (Cicero, 106–43 BC). "I'm not only a pacifist but a militant pacifist. I am willing to fight for peace. Nothing will end war unless the people themselves refuse to go to war" (Albert Einstein, 1931).

"There never was a good war, or a bad peace" (Ben Franklin, 1783). "War hath no fury like a noncombatant" (C. E. Montague, 1922). "Little girl . . . Sometime they'll give a war and nobody will come" (*The People, Yes* [1936] by Carl Sandburg, 1878–1967).

*Suppose They Gave a War and Nobody Came?* is the title of a 1970 film.

There is no way to peace; peace is the way.

David A. Hancock
Chester Township

# USA Has Had Addiction to War From Its First Days

To the editor:

In his State of the Union address, George W. (War) Bush neglected to mention that we are addicted to war along with oil. The greatest injustice is that the people who start the wars are not the ones who fight and die.

"To be prepared for war is one of the most effectual means of preserving peace," said George Washington in the first State of the Union address (Jan. 8, 1790). Washington's maxim has shaped United States policy ever since.

"Preparation for war is the surest guarantee for peace. I should welcome almost any war, for I think this country needs one," said Teddy Roosevelt.

"So long as anybody's terrorizing established governments, there needs to be a war," said George W. Bush.

"A nation is only at peace even if we have to fight for it," said Dwight D. Eisenhower.

"I want peace and I'm willing to fight for it," said Harry S. Truman.

"We make war that we may live in peace," said Aristotle.

"All diplomacy is a continuation of war by other means," said Zhou Enlai (1954).

"I know not with what weapons World War III will be fought, but World War IV will be fought with sticks and stones," said Albert Einstein.

"In fact, every war has been preceded by a peace conference. That's what always starts the next war," said Will Rogers.

"The object of war is not to die for your country, but to make the other bastard die for his," said Gen. George S. Patton.

"Political power grows out of the barrel of a gun," said Mao Tse-tung.

"The quickest way of ending a war is to lose it," said George Orwell.

"War! It's too serious a matter to leave to the military," said Georges Clemenceau.

At $1 million a minute since 1948, the United States has spent $15 trillion to build up its military might; $400 billion for 2004. Let's face it, there is no way to peace; peace is the way.

David A. Hancock
Chesterland

# Oppressive Tendencies

I'm thinking of the following people while writing this letter: George W. Bush, Dick Cheney, Karl Rove, John McCain, and Hillary and Bill Clinton.

Carol Tavris, social psychologist and author, states in *Mistakes Were Made (But Not by Me): Why We Justify Foolish Beliefs, Bad Decisions, and Hurtful Acts*, "Why do people dodge responsibility when things fall apart? Why the parade of public figures unable to own up when they screw up? Why the endless martial quarrels over who is right? Why can we see hypocrisy in others but not in ourselves? Are we all liars? Or do we really believe the stories we tell?"

Dr. Tavris takes a compelling look into how the brain is wired for self-justification and confabulation. When we make mistakes, we must calm the cognitive dissonance that jars our feelings of self-worth. And so we create fictions that absolve us of responsibility, restoring our belief that we are smart, moral and right—a belief that often keeps us on a course that is dumb, immoral and wrong.

*The Art of War* by Sun Tzu (and translated by Thomas Cleary) states that there are some basic principles that hurt the people:

- Officials who use public office for personal benefit, taking improper advantage of their authority, holding weapons in one hand and peoples' livelihood in the other, corrupting their offices and bleeding the people. There are cases where serious offenses are given light penalties. There is inequality before the law, and the innocent are subjected to punishment, even execution. Sometimes, serious crimes are pardoned, the strong are supported, and the weak are oppressed. Harsh penalties are applied, unjustly torturing people to get at facts.

- Sometimes there are officials who condone crime and vice, punishing those who protest against these, cutting off the avenues of appeal and hiding the truth, plundering and ruining lives, unjust and arbitrary.

- Sometimes there are senior officials who repeatedly change department heads so as to monopolize the government administration, favoring their friends and relatives, while treating those they dislike with unjust harshness, oppressive in their actions, prejudiced and unruly.

These things are harmful to the people, and anyone who does any of these should be dismissed from office.

All this reminds me of Lawrence W. Britt's research of the early warning signs of fascism: powerful and continuing nationalism, disdain for human rights, identification of enemies as a unifying cause, supremacy of the military, rampant sexism, controlled mass media, obsession with national security, religion and government intertwined, corporate power protected, labor power suppressed, disdain for intellectuals and the arts, obsession with crime and punishment, rampant cronyism and corruption, and fraudulent elections.

It sure seems that Edward Abbey was correct when he wrote, "A patriot must be ready to defend his country against his government."

Solipsism and pandering seem to reflect our present political culture. It's a scientific fact: scum always rises to the top.

David A. Hancock
Chesterland

# Letters to the Editor

## Goodness, Righteousness

I thought that I would change the topic from education to politics. I did some enlightening research on political oxymoronica and discovered Mardy Grothe's book *Oxymoronica: Paradoxical Wit and Wisdom from History's Greatest Wordsmiths*.

Paul Valery, the great French writer and critic, once wrote, "Politics is the art of preventing people from taking part in affairs which properly concern them." As with many wry comments, there's a great deal of truth embedded in his words.

According to Dr. Grothe, politicians throughout history, once in positions of power, have often been inclined to keep citizens away from the affairs of state. This is especially true when citizens are disgruntled and critical of the way things are being done. Sound familiar?

Let's take a look at and think about some other oxymoronica. "It is characteristic of the most stringent censorships that they give credibility to the opinions they attack" (Voltaire).

In Benjamin Disraeli's 1844 book *Coningsby*, he states, "No government can be long secure without formidable opposition." The weakest governments silence their opposition and, in so doing, have no adversaries to keep them on their toes. The strongest governments give their opposition a voice and, in theory at least, are willing to make changes necessary to govern more effectively, according to Dr. Grothe.

In 1790, the English statesman Edmund Burke said, "A state without some means of change is without the means of its conservation." The notion that governments must change to endure is at the heart of all great democracies.

In his 1954 book *Freedom, Loyalty, Dissent*, the American historian Henry Steel Commager said, "If our democracy is to flourish, it must have criticism; if our government is to function, it must have dissent." Like the Vietnam War and Iraq?

Sen. J. William Fulbright, of Arkansas, became one of the most vocal critics of American policy. In a 1966 speech to the American Newspaper Publishers Association, he gave an insight/view/ perspective as to how he felt about loyal dissent: "The citizen who criticizes his country is paying it an implied tribute."

One of the best examples was the Rev. Dr. Martin Luther King Jr. when he said, "An individual who breaks a law that conscience tells him is unjust, and who willingly accepts the penalty of imprisonment in order to arouse the conscience of the community over its injustice is in reality expressing the highest respect for the law." Dr. King was describing the time-honored concept of civil disobedience.

Our founding fathers recognized the potential for harm from those attempting to do good. In a letter to Thomas Jefferson, John Adams wrote, "Power always thinks it has a great soul and vast views beyond the comprehension of the weak, and that it is doing God's service, when it is violating all his laws."

Even when people are right in trying to do good, they can fail by overreaching, by attempting too much. The midterm elections of '06 sure seem to reflect some oxymoronica!

David A. Hancock
Chester

## Letters to the Editor

# IRAQ "EXPERTS" EXPOSED

Who said the war would pay for itself? They did!

The following quotes were compiled by Christopher Cerf and Victor Navasky in the capacity of chief executive officer and president of the Institute of Expertology, which has just issued a report on the experts who were wrong about Iraq—before, during, and after the invasion—under the title *Mission Accomplished! Or How We Won the War in Iraq: The Experts Speak* (Simon and Schuster). Here, the "experts" speak about the costs of war.

"Iraq is a very wealthy country. Enormous oil reserves. They can largely finance the reconstruction of their own country. And I have no doubt that they will" (Richard Perle, chairman, the Pentagon's Defense Policy Board, July 11, 2002).

"The likely economic effects [of a war, in Iraq] would be relatively small . . . Under every plausible scenario, the negative effect will be quite small relative to the economic benefits" (Lawrence Lindsey, White House economic adviser, Sept. 16, 2002).

"It is unimaginable that the United States would have to contribute hundreds of billions of dollars and highly unlikely that we would have to contribute even tens of billions of dollars" (Kenneth Pollack, former director for Persian Gulf affairs, National Security Council, September 2002).

"The costs of any intervention would be very small" (Glenn Hubbard, White House economic adviser, Oct. 4, 2002).

"Iraq has tremendous resources that belong to the Iraqi people. And so there are a variety of means that Iraq has to be able to shoulder much of the burden for their own reconstruction" (Ari Fleischer, White House press secretary, Feb. 18, 2003).

"When it comes to reconstruction, before we turn to the American taxpayer, we will turn first to the resources of the Iraqi government and the international community" (Donald Rumsfeld, secretary of defense, March 27, 2003).

"There is a lot of money to pay for this that doesn't have to be US taxpayer money, and it starts with the assets of the Iraqi people. We are talking about a country that can really finance its own reconstruction and relatively soon" (Paul Wolfowitz, deputy secretary of defense, testifying before the Defense Subcommittee of the House Appropriations Committee, March 27, 2003).

"The United States is very committed to helping Iraq recover from the conflict, but Iraq will not require sustained aid" (Mitchell Daniels, director, White House Office of Management and Budget, April 21, 2003).

"The allies [have contributed] $14 billion in direct aid" (Dick Cheney, vice presidential debate with Democratic candidate John Edwards, Oct. 5, 2004). Actually, only $13 billion was pledged, and on the date Mr. Cheney spoke, only $1 billion had arrived. As of October 28, 2007, the National Priorities Project estimated that the share of Iraq War costs that had been borne by American taxpayers exceeded $463 billion.

And of course, let us not forget the inveterate, confabulating verisimilitudes and malapropisms of Dick Cheney: "So?", "Go ——— yourself," and "I had other priorities than the military."

David A. Hancock
Chester

# Common Sense on Hiatus

Wow! The RNC in CLE! GOP (Greedy Old Party), OMG, WTF?

This reminds me of a cartoon poster on the office door of a political science colleague. On it was a picture of an elephant and a donkey. The caption defined bipartisanship: "I'll hug your elephant is you kiss my a——."

Fact: The states that the Republican National Committee chooses to have its convention votes Democratic 90 percent of the time. It's unfortunate that stupidity isn't painful. Oh well, Voltaire said, "Common sense is not so common."

Which reminds me that Sen. Sherrod Brown proposed legislation requiring that all American flags be made in the United States. Maybe we should also attach the following quote from Howard Zinn's *A People's History of the United States* and *The Historic Unfulfilled Promise*, "No flag is large enough to cover the shame of killing innocent people."

David A. Hancock
Chester

# Political Priorities

One of the gold medals of hubris should be presented to George W. Bush, who said, "I do not need to explain why I say things. That's the interesting thing about being president. Maybe somebody needs to explain to me why they say something, but I don't feel like I owe anybody an explanation."

However, I'll explain.

Some diabolical, didactic, pensive musings in reference to the letter "Dumbfounding Language" by Rory Althans (Aug. 7–8), which was in response to the letter "Common Sense on Hiatus" by David A. Hancock (July 24–25). Cartoons and political satire / sarcasm / parody and caricature are examples of expressions and opinions about attitudes, values, and philosophy. A blend of David Letterman, Bill Maher, Stephen Colbert, Jon Stewart, and Maureen Dowd are indelible representatives when it comes to commentaries on cultural mores and folkways.

I participated in army ROTC at Kent State University (1964–66). I decided not to be commissioned as a second lieutenant. Maybe my thinking was similar to George "Warmonger" Bush ("I'm the decider," or "A dictatorship would be a lot easier") and Dick "Shotgun Duckhunter" Cheney ("I have other priorities than the military"). Quack, quack!

Writer and critic Paul Valery wrote, "Politics is the art of preventing people from taking part in affairs which properly concern them." As with many wry oxymoronica comments, there's a great deal of truth embedded in Mr. Valery's thinking. Politicians, once in power, have often been inclined to keep citizens from the affairs of state. This is especially true when citizens are disgruntled and critical of the way things are being done. What to do with opponents and dissenters? How to silence critics? From censorship to assassination, etc.

However, such methods always prove to be ineffective in the long term. "It is characteristic of the most stringent censorships that they give credibility to the opinions they attack" (Voltaire). "No government can be long secure without formidable opposition" (Disraeli, 1844). And "A patriot must always be ready to defend his/her country against its government" (Edward Abbey).

(Acrimonious)

At Loggerheads Again

To Rory Althans: I do not hate our country. Although I do recall Mitt Romney ("Romnesia") say something about "self-deport." I visited Austria and Switzerland in July. As a first-year baby boomer, I have to admit that I really like Switzerland's politics and culture. However, I do not have a copious amount of money to deposit in their banks. WTF (wow, that's funny!)?

To all fellow denizens, read *The End of America: Letter of Warning to a Young Patriot* by Naomi Wolf.

Never forget that the most powerful weapon an oppressor has is the mind of the oppressed. For enlightenment, view *The Unknown Known* about Don Rumsfeld, where his brain is in a black hole. I would remind Rory Althans that Howard Zinn (1922–2010), author of many books including *A Power Governments Cannot Suppress*, saw combat duty as an air force bombardier in World War II.

David A. Hancock
Chester

# Letters to the Editor

## VOTING IS JUST A GAME

All voting is a sort of gaming, like checkers or backgammon, with a slight moral tinge to it, a playing with right and wrong, with moral questions; and betting naturally accompanies it. The character of the voters is not stacked. I cast my vote, perchance, as I think right but I am not vitally concerned that the right should prevail. I am willing to leave it to the majority. Its obligation, therefore, never exceeds that of expediency. Even voting for the right is doing nothing for it. It is only expressing to wo(man) feebly your desire that it should prevail. A wise wo(man) will not leave the right to the mercy of chance, nor wish it to prevail through the power of the majority.

There is but little virtue in the action of masses of wo(men). When the majority shall at length vote for the abolition of slavery, it will be because they are indifferent to slavery, or because there is but little slavery left to be abolished by their vote. They will then be the only slaves. Only his vote can hasten the abolition of slavery who asserts his own freedom by his vote. (Henry David Thoreau, 1849, *On the Duty of Civil Disobedience: Resistance to Civil Government*)

Today we may think of the following:

"Elections are won by men and women chiefly because most people vote against somebody rather than for somebody" (Franklin P. Adams, 1944).

"Hell, I never vote for anybody. I always vote against" (W. C. Fields).

"If voting changed anything, they'd abolish it" (Ken Livingstone, 1987).

Matt Lynch's maxim: "More jobs—less government." Advice to Matt Lynch: find a new job, new career, and do us all a favor and get out of government.

It's that time of year again. When I think of taxes, I think of the following perspicacity:

"I want to be sure that he is a ruthless SOB, that he will do what he is told, that every income-tax return I want to see, I see. That he will go after our enemies and not go after our friends. Now it's as simple as that. If he isn't, he doesn't get the job" (Richard Nixon on the kind of person he wanted to head the Internal Revenue Service).

"Read my lips: No new taxes" (George H. W. Bush).

"Only the little people pay taxes" (Leona Helmsley).

"Income tax has made more liars out of the American people than golf" (Will Rogers).

"There is no art which one government sooner learns of another than that of draining money from the pockets of the people" (*The Wealth of Nations* [1776], Adam Smith).

"The art of government is to make two-thirds of a nation pay all it possibly can pay for the benefit of the other third" (Voltaire, 1694–1778, attributed to Walter Bagehot's *The English Constitution* [1867]).

David A. Hancock
Chester

# Thoughts About Destiny

Novelist Dorothy Allison said, "Fiction is the great lie that tells the truth."

I thought about this and started to ruminate on human venal, sordid, narcissistic, and megalomaniacal behavior and attitudes, which then reminded me of Shakespeare's *Julius Caesar* and Mark Antony's speech that goes, "Friends, Romans, countrymen; lend me your ears. I come to bury Caesar, not praise him. The evil that men do lives after them. The good is oft interred with their bones. So let it be with Caesar." Now replace Caesar with some names that you can think of (e.g., dead dictators and living also).

This reflects a poster on a bulletin board at a local college counseling center, The Essence of Destiny:

> Watch your thoughts, for they become words. Choose
> your words, for they become actions. Understand your
> actions, for they become habits. Study your habits, for
> they become your character. Develop your character,
> for it becomes your destiny. (Anonymous)

Maybe Carl Sagan is right with his perspicacity: "I worry that . . . pseudoscience and superstition will seem year by year more tempting, the siren song of unreason more sonorous and attractive. Where have we heard it before? Whenever our ethnic or national prejudices are aroused, in times of scarcity, during challenges to national self-esteem or nerve, when we agonize about our diminished cosmic place and purpose or when fanaticism is bubbling up around us, then habits of thought familiar from ages past reach for the controls. The candle flame gutters. Its little pool of light trembles. Darkness gathers. The demons begin to stir."

David Hancock
Chester

# Politicians and Diapers

Cogitating about our discombobulating political quagmires and debacles—especially during the lame-duck, quack-quack Congress—reminds me of Eric Arthur Blair (a.k.a. George Orwell, 1946):

> We are all capable of believing things which we know to be untrue, and then, when we are finally proved wrong, impudently twisting the facts so as to show that we were right. Intellectually, it is possible to carry on this process for an indefinite time: The only check on it is that sooner or later a chimera (false belief) bumps up against solid reality, usually on a battlefield.

Sadly, it appears that many of these mendacious, Machiavellian knaves (politicians) cannot think clearly enough to understand that they are not thinking clearly. The problems we face will not be solved by the minds that created them. However, reading *One Nation: What We Can All Do to Save America's Future* by Ben Carson, MD, seems to be a panacea, in my opinion.

Maybe Will Rogers was correct when he said, "Things will get better despite our efforts to improve them." Or maybe Winston Churchill when he said, "Politics is the ability to foretell what is going to happen tomorrow, next week, next month and next year. And to have the ability afterwards to explain why it didn't happen." Or maybe Voltaire when he said, "Every wo(man) is the creature of the age in which s/he lives; very few are able to raise themselves above the ideas of the times."

Conclusion? Politicians and diapers need to be changed—often for the same reasons. What's the opposite of pro? Con! What's the opposite of progress? Congress!

David A. Hancock
Chester

# Laughter Happens Too

One of my colleagues, who teaches political philosophy, invited me to attend one of his classes. The assignment was for students to think of creative definitions with humor. It was based on some of the writings of Henry David Thoreau, the brilliant, unconventional, iconoclastic heretic.

I hope that we all enjoy some laughter. His students did not disappoint us. Here they are.

The religions:

- Taoism: ___ happens.
- Hinduism: This ___ has happened before.
- Confucianism: Confucius says, "___ happens."
- Zen: What is the sound of ___ happening?
- Islam: If ___ happens, it is the will of Allah.
- Jehovah's Witnesses: Knock, knock, ___ happens.
- Atheism: There is no such thing as ___.
- Agnosticism: Maybe ___ happens, and maybe not.
- Protestantism: ___ won't happen if I work harder.
- Catholicism: If ___ happens, I deserve it.
- Judaism: Why does ___ always happen to me?
- Televangelism: Send money or ___ will happen.

Politics:

- Conservative: The courts have allowed too much excrement.
- Independent: ___ happens.
- Democrat: ___ is a vast right-wing conspiracy.
- Republican: The rich deserve more ___.
- Moderate: We must also consider ___'s right to happen.
- Liberal: ___ will happen if we don't spend enough.
- Reform: We can't get our ___ in a group.
- Socialist: Support the equal distribution of ___.
- Communist: Come the revolution, ___ will not happen again.
- Libertarian: Legalize all kinds of ___.
- Green party: Compost happens.

There is no answer key.

David A. Hancock
Chester

# Faith Needs No Proof

I would like to settle the quagmire, debacle, ad infinitum, ad nauseam of the creationism-evolution debate written by several polemics during the past year.

Check out www.skeptic.com and read the following: "How to Debate a Creationist: 25 Creationist Arguments and 25 Evolutionist Answers for Enlightenment"; the Baloney Detection Kit; *Why People Believe Weird Things* and *How We Believe: The Search for God in an Age of Science*, both by Michael Shermer.

In conclusion, what is the relationship of science and religion? Evolution theory cannot replace faith and religion, and science has no interest in pretending that it can. The theory of evolution is a scientific theory, not a religious doctrine. It stands or falls on evidence alone. Religious faith, by definition, depends on belief when evidence is absent or unimportant. They fill different niches in the human psyche.

To fear the theory of evolution is an indication of a shortcoming in one's faith, as is looking to scientific proof for justification of one's religious beliefs. If creationists have true faith in their religion, it shouldn't matter what scientists think or say, and scientific proof of God or biblical stories should be of no interest.

Enough said. Now let's choose some other topics of interest and more important things to write about and discuss, OK? This nonsensical nonsense is nonsensical. Let's discuss taxes, war, jobs, community environment, human behavior disorders, education, parenting, politics, public policy, health, legal issues, etc.

"A union of Government and Religion tends to destroy Government and degrade Religion" (Justice Hugo Black, *Engel vs. Vitale*, 1962).

David A. Hancock
Chester

# Warning. Warning, Warning

The indelible *Warning to Patriots* by Naomi Wolf (social critic, political activist, cofounder of the Woodhill Institute for Ethical Leadership-American Freedom Campaign and author of *The End of America: Letter of Warning to a Young Patriot*) references the ten steps to a dictatorship: "All dictators: invoke an external threat; develop a paramilitary force; create a secret prison system; track ordinary citizens; arbitrarily detain and release them; harass citizens groups; target writers; intimidate the press; recast dissent as 'treason' and criticism as 'espionage' and eventually subvert the rule of law."

At times, in our own history, our commitment to freedom has faltered. The Alien and Sedition Act of 1793 made it a crime for Americans to speak critically—to "bring into contempt or disrepute"—of then-President John Adams and other US leaders. But Thomas Jefferson pardoned those convicted under these laws when he took office. During the Civil War, President Abraham Lincoln suspended habeas corpus, effectively declaring martial law in several states. Approximately forty thousand Americans were imprisoned by military authorities during the war, many for simply expressing their views. But when the war ended in 1865, the Supreme Court ruled it unconstitutional for military tribunals to try civilians.

Ruminating about these facts and reading *The End of America*, I thought about the following, which elicited cognitive dissonance:

"A patriot must be ready to defend his/her country against his/her government" (Edward Abbey).

"Those who make peaceful revolution impossible will make violent revolution inevitable" (John F. Kennedy).

"Dissent is the highest form of patriotism" (Howard Zinn).

"A dictatorship would be a lot easier. And without revealing the operating details of our (domestic spying) program, I just want to assure the American people that, one, I've got the authority to do this; two, it is a necessary part of my job to protect you; and three, we're guarding your civil liberties" (George W. Bush, White House press conference, Dec. 19, 2005).

"People need to watch what they say, watch what they do" (Ari Fleischer, former White House press secretary, 2001).

"Liberty, once lost, is lost forever" (John Adams, 1775).

"Make the lie big, make it simple, keep saying it, and eventually they will believe it" (Adolf Hitler).

"I believe there are more instances of the abridgement of the freedom of the people by gradual and silent encroachments of those in power than by violent and student usurpations" (James Madison, father of the Constitution, 1738).

"You can't have 100 percent security and then also have 100 percent privacy and zero inconvenience" (President Barack Obama).

Conclusion: "As nightfall does not come all at once, neither does oppression. In both instances, there is a twilight when everything remains seemingly unchanged. And it is in such a twilight that we all must be most aware of change in the air—however slight—lest we become unwitting victims of the darkness" (Justice William O. Douglas).

David A. Hancock
Chesterland

# A City Says No to Drones

On February 4, the city of Charlottesville became the first in the country to pass a resolution against the domestic use of drones. "The rapid implementation of drone technology throughout the United States poses a serious threat to the privacy and constitutional rights of the American people," the resolution states, calling for a two-year moratorium on drone technology. It also calls for "Congress and the general Assembly of the Commonwealth of Virginia to adopt legislation prohibiting information obtained from the domestic use of drones from being introduced into a Federal or State court, and precluding domestic use of drones equipped with antipersonnel devices, meaning any projectile, chemical, electrical, directed-energy (visible or invisible), or other device designed to harm, incapacitate, or otherwise negatively impact a human being."

As antiwar activist David Swanson points out, "The same City Council passed a resolution on January 17, 2012, calling for an end to drone wars, as well as ground wars, excessive military spending and any possible attack on Iran."*

David A. Hancock
Chesterland

---

\* *War Is a Lie* by David Swanson

# Of Religion and War

Mark Twain spent the last ten years of his life fighting against the US occupation of the Philippines as a member of the Anti-Imperialist League. It was during this time that he wrote some of his angriest essays, including *To the Person Sitting in Darkness* and *The War Prayer*. He was criticized for having lost his sense of humor.

*The War Prayer* was a biting satire written around 1905 during the US war in the Philippines. Twain was disgusted with the patriotic and religious fervor that motivated support for the war.

On a Sunday morning in a church filled with the faithful, the preacher prayed that God would bless the young soldiers, keep them strong in battle, encourage them in their patriotic work, and help them smite their foe.

Then an aged stranger, Twain, dressed in white robes, walked up to the preacher's side and spoke to the congregation. He explained that he was a messenger from God. "You have heard your servant's prayer—the uttered part of it. I am commissioned of God to put into words the other part of it—that part which the pastor—and also you in your hearts—fervently prayed, silently. Listen!"

### The War Prayer by Mark Twain

O Lord our father, our young patriots, idols of our hearts, go forth to battle—be thou near them. With them—in spirit—we also go forth from the sweet peace of our beloved firesides to smite the foe. O Lord our God, help us to tear their soldiers to bloody shreds with our shells, help us to cover their smiling fields with the pale forms of their patriot dead, help us to drown the thunder of the guns with the shrieks of their wounded, writhing in pain; help us to lay waste their humble homes with a hurricane of fire; help us to wring the hearts of their unoffending widows with unavailing grief; help us to turn them out rootless with little children to wander unfriended the wastes of the desolated land in rags and hunger and thirst, sports of the sun, flames of summer and the icy winds of winter, broken in spirit, worn with travail, imploring thee for the refuge of the grave and denied it—for our sakes who adore thee, Lord, blast their hopes, blight their lives, protract their bitter pilgrimage, make heavy their steps, water their way with their tears; stain the white snow with the blood of their wounded feet! We ask it, in the spirit of love, of him who is the source of love, and who is the ever faithful refuge and friend of all that are sore beset and seek his aid with humble and contrite hearts. Amen.

Mark Twain may still agree with what he said years earlier, "Nothing fails like prayer" (except *The War Prayer*) and "Faith is believing what you know ain't so."

He would probably agree with the sayings, "Religions are cults with more members" and "As my ancestors are free from slavery, I am free from the slavery of religion" (Butterfly McQueen).

He would probably join Freedom From Religion Foundation.

He would be singing the lyrics to "Give Peace a Chance" by John Lennon.

"May we never see another war. For in my opinion there never was a good war or a bad peace"(Ben Franklin, 1783).

Read; War is a lie.

by David Swanson

David A. Hancock
Chesterland

# Watch for False Alternatives

February was Presidents' Day and Black History Month. Our American government teacher, Mrs. Hotchkiss (1963–64), was very inspiring. I memorized President Lincoln's Gettysburg Address, the best short speech ever. I recall about 75 percent of the words now. Amazing! I read the speech again on Lincoln's birthday from *Lend Me Your Ears: Great Speeches in History* by William Safire.

I learned the following a few weeks ago from "The Great Debates" by Professor Patrick Grim, State University of New York at Stony Brook. As Lincoln said in the first of a series of debates with his rival Stephen Douglas, "Public sentiment is everything. With public sentiment, nothing can fail; without it, nothing can succeed."

Lincoln also said, "The best way to destroy an enemy is to make him a friend"; "This is a world of compensations; and he who would be no slave, must consent to have no slave"; "There is no reason in the world why the Negro is not entitled to all the natural rights enumerated in the Declaration of Independence, the right to life, liberty, and the pursuit of happiness."

And now the flip-flop statement by Lincoln: "I am not, nor ever have been, in favor of bringing about in any way the social and political equality of the white and black races (nor of making) voters or jurors of Negroes nor of qualifying them to hold office, nor to intermarry with white people."

Stephen Douglas said, "I believe this government was made by white men for the benefit of white men and their posterity forever, and

I am in favor of confining citizenship to white men, men of European birth and descent. Instead of conferring it upon Negroes, Indians and other inferior races."

For independent inquiry, look for a video of a recent debate online at Elections.NyTimes.com, select the video tab, then search for "presidential debates." Ask yourself, what precisely is the position? What precisely is the argument given? How good is that argument? Did the speaker commit any fallacies?

An example of a false alternative-dilemma fallacy is when a problem is presented as an either-or choice between two alternatives, when, in fact, those are not the only options.

Modern political philosophy: false alternatives.

"Either you're with us, or you're with the terrorists" (Former President George W. Bush).

"Either we cut education and medical research, or we've got to reform the tax code so that the most profitable corporations have to give up tax loopholes that other companies don't get. We can't afford to do both" and "Either we ask the wealthiest Americans to pay their fair share in taxes, or we're going to have to ask seniors to pay more for Medicare. We can't afford to do both" (President Barack Obama).

Assignment: Read *What's Race Got to Do with It?: Why It's Time to Stop the Stupidest Argument in America* by Larry Elder and *The Miseducation of Black Children* by Kmt Shockley.

David A. Hancock
Chester

# Delusions Deserve Scorn

Emil Marino stated in another publication, "My pick would be Mike Huckabee. He has shown how very well informed he is on all subjects that affect our lives."

Mr. Huckabee's book *God, Guns, Grits, and Gravy* is No. 4 on the New York Times bestseller list. I wonder if Mr. Marino agrees and if Mr. Huckabee recalls his odious comment on Jan. 25, published by Planned Parenthood, "Women are helpless without Uncle Sugar coming in and providing for them a prescription each month for birth control because they cannot control their libido without the help of government."

Maybe Mr. Huckabee viewed or attended a performance of Eve Ensler's *The Vagina Monologues.* Maybe he could produce *The Penis Monologues* or *The Viagra-Cialis Chronicles.* I'm glad it's not Ed Huckabee.

How do we discuss/debate rationally with someone who holds such delusional beliefs? Maybe give up on reason and resort to excoriating ridicule, scorn and lampoons.

The ability of the human brain to convince itself of just about anything is not to be underestimated. Let's hope Will Rogers was correct when he said, "Things will get better despite our efforts to improve them."

Mr. Huckabee has three other colleagues who have similar views: "Women's voices are not appropriate or qualified to participate in the debate over birth control" (Rep. Darrell Issa, R–Calif.); "That's not denying women's rights. If a woman then wants birth control, go work somewhere else" (Kansas Gov. Sam Brownback); "If it's a legitimate rape, the female body has ways to shut that whole thing down" (Former Rep. Todd Akin, R–Mo.).

WOW—War on Women—and the "Pander Bears" have spoken. It's enough to make a cat laugh.

If any of the above miscreants are married, their spouses-partners have grounds for divorce.

Homework reading assignment: *The Joy of Not Being Married: A Guide to Singles (And Those Who Wish They Were)* by Ernie Zelinski and *No Kids: 40 Good Reasons Not to Have Children* by Corinne Maier.

Madeleine de Scudery probably said it best when she said, "In losing a husband, one loses a master who is often an obstacle to the enjoyment of many things." And Liz Winston who said, "I think, therefore, I am single" may have been referring to George Washington, who said, "It's better to be alone than with bad company."

David A. Hancock
Chester

# Football Proficiency Law

Here's the No Child Left Behind football version.

All teams must make the state playoffs, and all must win the championship. If a team does not win the championship, they will be on probation until they are the champions and coaches will be held accountable. If, after two years, they have not won the championship, their footballs and equipment will be taken away until they do win the championship.

All kids will be expected to have the same football skills at the same time, even if they do not have the same conditions or opportunities to practice on their own. No exceptions will be made for lack of interest in football, a desire to perform athletically, or genetic abilities or disabilities of themselves or their parents. All kids will play football at a proficient level.

Talented players will be asked to work out on their own, without instruction. This is necessary because the coaches will be using all their instructional time with the athletes who aren't interested in football. Games will be played year round, but statistics will only be kept on the third, fourth, fifth, eighth and tenth games.

It will create a new age of sports where every school is expected to have the same level of talent and all teams will reach the same minimum goals. If no child gets ahead, then no child gets left behind.

If parents do not like this new law, they are encouraged to vote for vouchers and support private schools that can screen out the nonathletes and prevent their children from having to go to school with bad football players.

This law has been revised from *A Teacher's Calendar—Didactic Pensive Musings, Satire, and Oxymorons on Education Issues.*

Where is it said that everything worth learning is on a test?

David A. Hancock
Chester

## Letters to the Editor

# WIT AND WISDOM TO PONDER

Dave Lange's perspicacious column and uninvited commencement address, "Graduates Get Words of Wisdom," of June 4–5, "I'm Going to Tell You What Not to Do," reminded me of my commencement address as senior class adviser to the class of 1987 at Cleveland Heights High School.

Ruminating on the event at the Front Row Theatre with approximately 2,500 in attendance, my introduction was, "I have a gift to the graduating class of 1987. My speech will be short." Laughter. "As all of you know, being a science educator, I do not want to add excess carbon dioxide to the atmosphere and damage ozone."

The title of my commencement address should have been "I'm Going to Tell You What You Should Do."

"Please refer to the additional supplemental references in your program for future reference. Refer to it frequently. So you don't have to take notes now and take a test on Monday." Laughter.

Thank your inspiring teachers. Verbally and written.

Overcome your miseducation. By this, I mean what was educationally significant and hard to measure seems to be replaced by what is educationally insignificant and easy to measure—multiple guess-memory tests. So now we measure how well we're taught what isn't worth learning.

Remember the following wit and wisdom:

- "I never let schooling interfere with my education" (Mark Twain).
- "You can get all As and still flunk life" (Marian Wright Edelman).
- "Fame-celebrity is a mask that eats into the face" (John Updike).

Avoid the lethal habits of criticizing, blaming, complaining, nagging, bullying, threatening, punishing, bribing, and controlling.

Good judgment comes from experience. Experience comes from bad judgment. Read *Mistakes Were Made (But Not by Me): Why We Justify Foolish Beliefs, Bad Decisions, and Hurtful Acts* by Carol Tavris and Elliot Aronson.

Avoid the lethal need to judge, to keep score, to get even, to control.

Practice the caring habits of supporting, encouraging, listening (listen and silent have the same letters), accepting, trusting, respecting, and negotiating differences. Avoid being a misanthrope.

Do not be odious, petulant, or a boss-dictator. Be a leader who does not fix blame but fixes mistakes.

Read and implement *The No Asshole Rule* by Robert Sutton.

The quality of our life is determined by the quality of our thinking.

Avoid the mistakes of humans recommended by Marcus Tullius Cicero (106–43 BC), which are the illusion that personal gain is made up of crushing others, neglecting development and refinement of the mind and not acquiring the habit of reading and study, and attempting to compel others to believe and live as we do.

Read and study the following ASAP:

- *30 Days to Better Thinking and Better Living through Critical Thinking: A Guide for Improving Every Aspect of Your Life* by Linda Elder and Richard Paul

- *Wisdom of the Ages: A Modern Master Brings Eternal Truths into Everyday Life* by Wayne Dyer
- Any *Don't Sweat the Small Stuff* books by Richard Carlson
- Any book by Rabbi Harold Kushner, especially *Living a Life that Matters* and *Overcoming Life's Disappointments: Learning from Moses How To Cope With Frustration*
- *Too Soon Old, Too Late Smart: Thirty True Things You Need to Know Now* by Gordon Livingston, MD
- *Believing Bullshit: How Not to Get Sucked into an Intellectual Black Hole* by Stephen Law
- *The Five Secrets You Must Discover Before You Die* by John Izzo
- *The Top Ten Things Dead People Want to Tell You* by Mike Dooley

David A. Hancock
Chester

# Final Reflections

"If Hancock elicits anger, he should at least make you think, and that is always a good precedent for action."

### The Problem

School is the first place where children learn how to fail. School culture (physical and psychological environments) tends to elicit and are antecedents to student oppositional defiant disorder (especially if you are a boss-dictator who manages and teaches with coercion.

### The Solution

As Kirsten Olson reports in her book *Wounded by School: Recapturing the Joy in Learning and Standing Up to Old School Culture:*

> We all have to start by actually noticing, in a clear and relatively objective way, the things that are dysfunctional about school: how it's organized, how it makes learners feel day to day, how it achieves its "results" and whether those results are the ones we actually want and intend. Lots of us involved with school teachers, students, parents, administrators, support staff, policymakers—complain about

educational systems, but don't take action to join together with others to actually do something about them. The Giant Step in standing up is forming groups to begin talking to others about school practices, policies, and procedures that don't work— groups that help us understand why schools are as they are, and what we can do about them. Standing up often involves starting with small acts of protest, asking hard questions, supporting others in objecting, refusing to accept "Because that's the way we do it" answers. Seemingly insignificant little changes can lead to big transformations. It's a matter of getting started. Otherwise, it's an oxymoron; "It is essential to the triumph of Reform that it should never succeed."

William Hazlitt, English writer

My intentions are to be a provocateur who uses words to fulminate discussion, debate, deliberation, and introspection in reference to teaching, learning, schooling, and education.

I recall one of my colleagues saying that we should evaluate a book by whether we can remember them or whether they change the way we think/feel about an issue or subject. It is my hope that I have changed the way you think and feel about teaching, learning, schooling, and education. "We must be the change we wish to see in the world" (Gandhi).

# The Panacea

1. We need more male (especially black male) teachers K–5. As it stands now, 83 percent of teachers are white women and 93 percent of K–5 teachers are white women.
2. Administration needs to appoint teachers who reflect the "distinctive dispositions and temperaments—personality characteristics of successful teachers."
3. Teachers/educators need to implement the philosophy of Haim Ginott in *Teacher and Child* and *Between Parent and Child,* William Glasser in *The Quality School Teacher,* and Jawanza Kunjufu (AfricanAmericanImages.com) in *Black Students. Middle Class Teachers*, and Kmt Shockley in *The Miseducation of Black Children.*
4. Sadly, I think that many cannot think clearly enough to understand that they are not thinking clearly in reference to teaching, learning, schooling, and education.
5. In order to teach children fairly and equally, we must treat and teach them differently. Is it a learning disability or a teaching disability?
6. The indelible words of Arthur Costa—"What was educationally significant and hard to measure has been replaced by what is educationally insignificant and easy to measure. So now we measure how well we've taught what isn't worth learning."
7. Let's replace the educationally insignificant to the educationally significant!

## Appendix A

## BEHAVIOR MANAGEMENT REFLECTIONS

Instructions: Write the paragraph assigned by the end of class the next school day. Failure to do so will result in a more severe form of reprimand.

*****************************************************

I was given this short paragraph to write as a reminder not to use profanity in the classroom, a violation of school policy and classroom rules. I must demonstrate more self-control and discipline in the weeks ahead. I appreciate this method and this approach to deal with my social and personal development as a responsible young adult. I understand that if this disciplinary action does not appear to control my use of profanity in the classroom, a more severe form of reprimand will follow. However, by demonstrating self-control and discipline, I will not receive another paragraph for profanity and will be able to use my time more efficiently in activities that develop my academic potential and my intellectual growth.

*****************************************************

I was given this short paragraph to write as a reminder not to use racially / nationality insulting terms in the classroom, a violation of school policy and classroom rules. I must demonstrate more self-control and discipline in the weeks ahead. I appreciate this method and this approach to deal with my social and personal development as a responsible young adult. I understand that if this disciplinary action does not appear to control my use of racially / nationality insulting terms in the classroom, a more severe form of reprimand will follow. However, by demonstrating self-control and discipline, I will not receive another paragraph for racially / nationality insulting terms and will be able to use my time more efficiently in activities that develop my academic potential and my intellectual growth.

\*\*\*\*\*\*\*\*\*\*\*\*\*\*\*\*\*\*\*\*\*\*\*\*\*\*\*\*\*\*\*\*\*\*\*\*\*\*\*\*\*\*\*\*\*\*\*\*\*\*\*\*\*\*\*\*\*\*\*\*\*

I was given this short paragraph to write as a reminder not to disrupt the educational atmosphere, a violation of school policy and classroom rules. I must demonstrate more self-control and discipline in the weeks ahead. I appreciate this method and this approach to deal with my social and personal development as a responsible young adult. I understand that if this disciplinary action does not appear to control my disruption in the classroom, a more severe form of reprimand will follow. However, by demonstrating more self-control and discipline, I will not receive another paragraph for disruption of the classroom and will be able to use my time more efficiently in activities that develop my academic potential and my intellectual growth.

\*\*\*\*\*\*\*\*\*\*\*\*\*\*\*\*\*\*\*\*\*\*\*\*\*\*\*\*\*\*\*\*\*\*\*\*\*\*\*\*\*\*\*\*\*\*\*\*\*\*\*\*\*\*\*\*\*\*\*\*\*

## Appendix B

# THE EDUCATOR'S OATH

I solemnly pledge to dedicate my life to the science of teaching. I will give to those who are or have been my teachers the respect and gratitude which is their due. I will practice my profession with conscience and dignity: the well-being of my students will be my primary concern always. I will honor the position of parents and uphold public trust. I will maintain by all the means in my power. (Robert L. DeBruyn, author of *The Master Teacher*)

I meditated on this oath daily since I started teaching in 1969! The placebo effect?

## Appendix C

# Eleven Ways to Raise
# a Toxic Child

**by Bill Oliver**

> Reprinted with permission from the Passage
> Group (www.thepassagegroup.com).

1. **Be their lawyer.** No matter what they do, defend them. Be their advocate . . . right or wrong.
2. **Be their banker.** Finance all of their wants. This will give them a sense of entitlement which will last them for the rest of their lives.
3. **Be their insurance company.** Any time they make a mistake, you pay the price. They have the party . . . you have the hangover.
4. **Be their agent.** Cut the best deals for them. Use your personal contacts and influence to be sure that they rise to the top.
5. **Be their mechanic.** If anything in their life is broken, you fix it . . . even if they broke it themselves. That way, they will never have to learn about "consequences."
6. **Be their administrative assistant.** Every child needs a personal secretary. Be sure to let them delegate their

responsibilities to you. Always do their homework for them . . . that way, they can make the "honor roll."

7. **Be their butler.** Learning how to manage servants will be important as they grow up and become successful. Let them start with you.

8. **Be their apologist.** Put your best "spin" forward. Make excuses for their bad behavior. Blame the teacher, the school, the community, the Republicans, the Democrats . . . anybody but your child.

9. **Be their emotional doormat.** They have a bad day and you pay the price. They want respect from everyone but refuse to give it to you.

10. **Be their fairy godparent.** Turn pumpkins into coaches. Wave your wand and make it happen. After all, making them "happy" is your primary function in life.

11. **Fail to share your belief system with your child.** They will have a system of belief. The question becomes "Who will teach it to them, and what will it be?" People act out of what they believe . . . in their hearts. The difference between Hitler and Mother Theresa was a matter of belief. Like the song from the musical *South Pacific* says, "You Have to Be Carefully Taught."

# Further Reading List

- Don't forget to look up the word *heterodoxy* and then follow the meaning during the rest of your life.
- *The Mad Teacher panacea.* Let's settle this once and for all—right here, right now. Become an autodidact and read/review/reflect on the following: "What The Teacher is—is more important than what s/he teaches" (Karl Menninger).
- *The Quality School Teacher* and *Every Student Can Succeed* by William Glasser (wglasser.com).
- *Heart of a Teacher* by Paula J. Fox.
- *Wounded by School: Recapturing the Joy in Learning and Standing Up to Old School Culture* by Kirsten Olson.
- *Endangered Minds: Why Children Don't Think and What We Can Do About It* by Jane M. Healy.
- *The Inspired Teacher: How to Know One, Grow One, or Be One* by Carol Frederick Steele.
- *The American Public School Teacher: Past, Present, and Future* by Darrel Drury and Justin Baer.
- Any publication from RethinkingSchools.org and journal subscription.
- Any publication from AfricanAmericanImages.com.
- Any publication from ASCD.org professional development DVDs.
- Any publication from ResponsiveClassroom.org.
- Any publication from MasterTeacher.com.

- Any publication from TeachersCollege/tcpress.com.
- *Black Students. Middle Class Teachers* by Jawanza Kunjufu.
- *Challenging Assumptions in Education: From Institutionalized Education to a Learning Society* by Wendy Priesnitz (The Alternate Press).
- *In Their Own Way: Discovering and Encouraging Your Child's Personal Learning Style* by Thomas Armstrong.
- *The Myth of the A.D.D. Child: 50 Ways to Improve Your Child's Behavior and Attention Span without Drugs, Labels, or Coercion* by Thomas Armstrong.
- *Dumbing Us Down: The Hidden Curriculum of Compulsory Schooling* by John Taylor Gatto.
- *Motivating Black Males to Achieve in School and in Life* by Baruti Kafele.
- *Black Teachers on Teaching* by Michele Foster.
- *Teaching with Poverty in Mind* by Eric Jensen.
- *50 Ways to Close the Achievement Gap (3$^{rd}$ Ed.)* by Downey, et al.
- *Smart Parenting for African Americans: Helping Your Kids Thrive in a Difficult World* by Jeffrey Gardere.
- *Young, Gifted and Black* by Michelle Foster.
- *Dead Poets Society* (movie featuring Robin Williams).
- Teaching Tolerance (Tolerance.org).
- TheGreatCourses.com.
- "The Intelligent Brain" by Richard J. Haier (TheGreatCourses. com/course/642).
- *Closing the Racial Academic Achievement Gap* by Matthew Lynch.
- *Raising Black Students' Achievement through Culturally Responsive Teaching* by Johnnie McKinley (AlfieKohn.org).
- *The Homework Myth: Why Our Children Are Getting Too Much of a Bad Thing* by Alfie Kohn.
- *Feel-Bad Education: And Other Contrarian Essays on Children and Schooling* by Alfie Kohn.

- *The End of Homework: How Homework Disrupts Families, Overburdens Children, and Limits Learning* by Etta Kralovec and John Buell.
- *What Happened to Recess and Why Are Our Children Struggling in Kindergarten?* by Susan Ohanian.
- *One Size Fits Few* by Susan Ohanian.
- *What Successful Teachers Do: 101 Research-Based Classroom Strategies for New and Veteran Teachers* by Neal A. Glasgow.
- *The Don't Sweat Guide For Teachers; Cutting Through The Clutter So that Every Day Counts* by Richard Carlson.
- *Smart Kids, Bad Schools: 38 Ways to Save America's Future* by Brian Crosby.
- *Braking Free from Myths About Teaching and Learning Innovation As An Engine for Student Success* by Allison Zmuda.
- *Wasting Minds: Why Our Education System Is Failing and What We Can Do About It* by Ronald A. Wolk.
- *Motivating Students Who Don't Care: Successful Techniques for Educators* by Allen N. Mendler.
- *Why Schools Fail* by Bruce Goldberg.
- *The Queen of Education: Rules for Making School Work* by LouAnne Johnson.
- *The Hurried Child* by David Elkind.
- *We Can't Teach What We Don't Know: White Teachers, Multiracial Schools (2ⁿᵈ Ed.)* by Gary Howard.
- *Raising Race Questions: Whiteness and Inquiry in Education* by Ali Michael.
- *The Culturally Inclusive Educator: Preparing for a Multicultural World* by Dena Samuels.
- *Why Race and Culture Matter in Schools: Closing the Achievement Gap in America's Classrooms* by Tyrone E. Howard.
- *Bad Teachers: How Blaming Teachers Distorts the Bigger Picture* by Kevin K. Kumashiro.

- *A Handbook for Teachers of African American* Children by Baruti Kafele.
- "The Futurist, Forecasts, Trends and Ideas About the Future Educations Holy Grail: Personalized Learning" by Maria H. Andersen, wfs.org (Jan/Feb 2011).
- *Frames of Mind and Multiple Intelligences* by Howard Gardner.
- *The Scientist in the Crib: Minds, Brains, and How Children Learn* by Alison Gopnik.
- *The Teacher Wars: A History of America's Most Embattled Profession* by Dana Goldstein.
- *Deschooling Society* by Ivan Illich.
- *The Teenage Liberation Handbook* by Grace Llewellyn.
- *Get Over It! Education Reform Is Dead. Now What?* by Caren Black.
- *Beyond the Classroom: Why School Reform Has Failed and What Parents Need To Do* by Laurence Steinberg.
- *I Hate School: How to Help Your Child Love Learning* by Cynthia Wrich Tobias.
- *The Death of Common Sense of Our Schools and What You Can Do About It* by Jim Grant.
- *Inspirational Quotes Notes and Anecdotes That Honor Teachers and Teaching* by Robert D. Ramsey.
- National Professional Resources (NPRinc.com).
- *High Schools, Race, and America's Future: What Students Can Teach Us About Morality, Diversity, and Community* by Lawrence Blum.

Not being a polymath teacher, Hancock communicates his vision, experiences, opinions, philosophy, perceptions, and beliefs about teaching, learning, and education issues in society with vibrant energy, passion, and verve.

Satire, parody, and caricatures are also included.

Anyone interested in the state of education will want to read and think (reflect) about Hancock's eclectic pontifications and jeremiads in reference to education policies, practices, and procedures.

Hancock's moniker is the Don Quixote of Educational Philosophy.

Hancock after retirement (2003) conducts/presents professional development seminars at local colleges / school districts on the achievement gap and is an education consultant / child advocate. See flyer/brochure on page ___.

He had a professional educator career from 1968 to 2003.

You Can Handle Them All—Strategies to Reduce/Narrow the Academic Achievement Gap. Problems, Causes, Solutions: Moving from Research to Practice

David Hancock, MA

| | |
|---|---|
| Dates: | August 5 and 6, 2014 |
| | (Attendance is required at all sessions) |
| Times: | 9:00 a.m.–4:00 p.m. |
| Location: | NDC Administration Building |
| | (Room signs will be posted) |

There is no single achievement gap. However, there are many kinds of gaps (i.e., attitude, racial, teacher quality, poverty, environment, etc.) The achievement gap has been a long-standing issue in US public education. To date, no programs or approaches have erased it, although some actions have shown promise to conceptualize the multidimensional nature of the gap issue and help define the means by which educators can begin to implement strategies to attack it successfully. This seminar is a trenchant analysis of the topics that are promoted by AfricanAmericanImages.com with usable resources and proposals for action.

| | |
|---|---|
| Graduate credit: | 1 semester hour |
| Graduate course no.: | ED526A |
| Graduate course cost: | $260 |

Solving Academic and Behavioral Problems

ADHD Diagnosis: Coerced to take Ritalin?
You can get all As and still flunk life.

Was just informed that pre-K testing will begin and no recess!

Cure for Pain? No Brain Drugs.

- "The ADD/ADHD Checklist" by Sandra Rief
- *Non-Drug Treatments for ADHD* by Brown and Gerbarg
- *Parenting Children with ADHD* by Monastra
- *ADHD*, American Academy of Pediatrics
- *ADHD for Dummies* by Strong and Flanagan
- *ADD/ADHD Alternatives in the Classroom* by Armstrong
- *The ADD/ADHD Answer Book: The Top 275 Questions Parents Ask* by Ashley
- ADHD report by Guildford (Add.org)

What the teacher is is more important than what she/he teaches.

Positive Traits Common in Many Children and Adults with ADHD

- Energetic
- Creative
- Innovative
- Risk-taker
- Good-hearted
- Accepting and forgiving
- Resilient
- Gregarious
- Humorous
- Willing to take a chance and try new things
- Able to find novel solutions
- Observant

- Can think on their feet
- Can make and create fun
- Ready for action
- Enthusiastic
- Spontaneous
- Persistent
- Imaginative
- Tenacious
- Ingenuity
- Inquisitive
- Resourceful
- Not boring
- Outgoing
- Good at improvising
- Inventive
- Full of ideas and spunk
- Good in crisis situations
- Enterprising
- Intelligent and bright
- Know how to enjoy the present

Schools should not be urgent day care, psychiatric trauma centers, and satellite orphanages with borderline and antisocial personality disorders as clients!

Recommended Reading:

- *Kids on Meds* by Kalikow
- AskTheJudge.Info (Children and the Law)
- Students Against Destructive Decisions (SADD.org, 877-723-3462)
- ActiveParenting.com
- TheGreatCourses.com (800-832-2412)
- How We Learn Course No. 1691

- Scientific Secrets for Raising Kids Who Thrive Course No. 9542
- Raising Emotionally and Socially Healthy Kids Course No. 9531
- *What Do You Really Want for Your Children?* by Wayne Dyer
- Carson Scholars Fund by Ben Carson, MD (CarsonScholars.org)
- Education consultant services / interventions
- Education advocate / consultant: Helps to facilitate communication between parents and schools/teachers. I can assist the parents of children (K–12) with education issues, such as ADHD, learning, emotional, and behavioral issues, with home visits and school visits / conferences. Forty years experience.
- I can help you manage the quagmire of school bureaucracy. I will make them listen to reason!

Call me: David A. Hancock, MA
Phone No.: 440-487-0829

WJCU 88.7 FM: The Diary of a Mad Professor (iconoclastic, heretic, gadfly) palaver, wry, pedagogue, and erudite, pontifications, diatribes, harangues, and demagoguery with personal musings, ruminations, lamentations, and VIPs (views, insights, and perspectives) about the state of schooling and education in the United States.

The Mad Professor is an avant-garde and bellwether when it comes to the conundrums of education.

The Mad Professor uses parody, satire, and caricatures in his explanations about what is wrong with our education system today. He is definitely a bon vivant and raconteur when it comes to schooling and education. As Mark Twain said, "I never let schooling interfere with my Education."

Cutting-edge research and innovative best practices share ideas and experiences and education knowledge to drive school reform!

You will become addicted to the Mad Professor! He is fervent and unequivocal with his philosophy and message about education issues!

Professor monologues: twelve/thirty minute harangues.

Printed in the United States
By Bookmasters